Contributions to Management Science

The series *Contributions to Management Science* contains research publications in all fields of business and management science. These publications are primarily monographs and multiple author works containing new research results, and also feature selected conference-based publications are also considered. The focus of the series lies in presenting the development of latest theoretical and empirical research across different viewpoints.

This book series is indexed in Scopus.

More information about this series at http://www.springer.com/series/1505

Vu Quang Trinh

Fundamentals of Board Busyness and Corporate Governance

Springer

Vu Quang Trinh
Newcastle University Business School
Newcastle University
Newcastle Upon Tyne, UK

ISSN 1431-1941 ISSN 2197-716X (electronic)
Contributions to Management Science
ISBN 978-3-030-89227-2 ISBN 978-3-030-89228-9 (eBook)
https://doi.org/10.1007/978-3-030-89228-9

This Springer imprint is published by the registered company Springer Nature Switzerland AG.
The registered company address is: Gewerbestrasse 11, 6330 Cham, Switzerland

"This is a timely and pertinent book which deals with the topical subject matter of busyness of boards in a more thorough and comprehensive manner than it has been done hitherto. It scrutinizes how busyness impacts on the banking sector through the application of modern financial concepts and methods. This book will be of equal importance to students of finance who would appreciate it as a textbook and researchers who will gain deeper insights on the subject from the cutting-edge analysis provided."
—**Professor Neelu Seetaram**, *Professor, Leeds Beckett University, United Kingdom*

"The very comprehensive review on the financial outcomes of banks with busy directors within modern corporate governance in the banking sector. The handbook is extremely helpful for those students and early career researchers who intend to attain high level of knowledge in the field of governance and board busyness. Readers will find this book very informative in understanding the theoretical issues around board busyness and financial outcomes in the global banking system, for both Islamic and conventional banks. The corporate reformers such as the National Association of Corporate Directors (2012) questioned that too many board positions will lead to bad corporate governance quality and in turn, lower financial outcomes. Therefore, there is no doubt that the idea of board busyness with limited time and attention inclined to bad corporate governance practices, based on the 'agency theory,' has generated a set of financial outcomes in the banking system. It is probably one of the best and most comprehensive handbooks of 'board busyness' ever seen in corporate governance."
—**Dr Chi Keung Marco Lau**, *Senior Lecturer in Economics, Teesside University, United Kingdom*

"The author is an enthusiastic, dedicated, and devoted researcher, who always 'crave for knowledge' with unstoppable creative exploration in the fields of corporate finance and corporate governance. It is a delight to commend Trinh's latest book *Fundamentals of Board Busyness and Corporate Governance*. When it comes to a

critical governance topic on board busyness, Trinh can confidently take the lead with an abundance of credible and published works on very highly and internationally acknowledged journals. The book covers thoroughly many important aspects of the subject looking from both theoretical and empirical perspectives, taking the readers from the surface to a deep level of understanding about the board busyness and its impacts on corporations. Most importantly, the book encompasses a very unique context of dual banking system including conventional and Islamic banks, whose governance structures are distinct. This provides academic and professional readers with useful insights into the criticality of board busyness in different institutional management operations."
—**Dr Rosie Cao**, *Lecturer in Accounting & Finance, Bath University, United Kingdom*

"This is a brilliant and timely book. The book has provided rigorous evidence regarding whether and to what extent the multiple directorships of board members can generate a meaningful impact on various corporate outcomes for different banking firms. Academic studies are rarely easy to read, but now the author has made his work accessible to a broader audience and explain academic evidence in an interesting and reader-friendly manner. This is a must-read book for anyone interested in how financial firms can improve corporate governance to make long-term value for not only shareholders but also all relevant stakeholders in our society. PhD students and early career researchers are highly recommended to keep it as a pocketbook. I am sure it will comfort your nerve at the very beginning of your research journey."
—**Dr Teng Li**, *Lecturer in Accounting & Finance, Newcastle University, United Kingdom*

"This book offers a thorough knowledge of board busyness and corporate governance by a talented and dedicated researcher in the field. With influential theoretical frameworks, pertinent empirical evidence, and an in-depth discussion of board busyness research, this book would be a must-read for anyone fascinated about the topics."
—**Dr Hang Nguyen**, *Lecturer in Management, Huddersfield University, United Kingdom*

"*Fundamentals of Board Busyness and Corporate Governance* is a fascinating and important book, written in engaging styles and packed with important theories and concepts on banking system. A must-read book for every student and new researcher interested in this field."
—**Dr Emily Ngan Luong**, *Senior Lecturer in Marketing, London South Bank University, United Kingdom*

To You

My Dad,
Trinh Quang Thanh

and

My Mom,
Tran Thi Thu The

Preface

Understanding the possible effects of "busy" directors (i.e., who hold multiple directorships) is a fundamental subject within modern corporate governance, board management, and financial-related fields. Conventionally, several standard corporate governances and financial theories and models have been established to study and evaluate director and corporate behaviors in terms of risk-taking and decision-making, and in turn, financial stability, market valuations, and policies. Remarkably, current practices of governance in the financial services sector differ from their non-financial counterparts in either form or substance or both. Like traditional businesses, agency conflicts within banks can also occur under the condition of separation of ownership and control. The principals (owners or shareholders) try, through employing several governance mechanisms, to minimize these high costs and protect their interests. The governance of banks, however, is expected in principle to be unique due to their higher complexity and different structure of balance sheets compared to industrial firms. Their context of intense regulation and greater asymmetry leads to the special relevance and roles of the board of directors whose responsibilities are to approve a bank's policies, procedures, and business strategies as well as has ultimate oversight responsibility for corporate decisions.

The duties of obligations of the bank (inside and outside) directors serving on the board may arise in two main contexts: a discrete decision brought to the board for approval that increases directors' legal responsibility on the bank safety and soundness and their obligation to provide firm oversight on whose boards they serve. Alongside their advisory roles, directors are also expected to provide vigilant oversight over executives and perform their duties independently from insiders. They should serve as monitors on inside board members and managers on behalf of capital providers, and, as a result, are anticipated to mitigate the agency conflicts. To monitor managers effectively, those directors are expected to invest their time and attention to analyze any key information provided by management boards (which includes chief executive officers—CEOs), financial intermediates, as well as consultants. Also, some stakeholders (e.g., authorities) have placed additional expectations on a bank's board of directors that delineate their responsibilities even further. As a result, the role of the board of directors in banking institutions becomes central in its governance structure. Such uniqueness of the governance in the banks, therefore, implies a dominant effect of the board of directors on the corporate decisions and outcomes.

Resource dependence theorists argue that holding too many directorships of directors, which is a common phenomenon in modern businesses occurring when these directors serve in three or more organizations, may have some reputational benefits to the board advising and monitoring effectiveness. Such "busy" individuals should have superior knowledge, skills, rich experience, and wide networking, which contributes to enhancing corporate value in the eyes of stakeholders. However, in recent years, an increasing amount of empirical evidence has criticized that such reputational benefits of board "busyness" cannot be sustained in practice. Indeed, institutional investors and shareholder activists argue another side effect of this board is that "busy" directors are incapable of effectively advising and monitoring managers of too many organizations at the same time. Likewise, corporate reformers such as the National Association of Corporate Directors (2012) and the Council of Institutional Investors (2012) both suggest limiting the number of board seats held by directors. The former recommends that a director should hold no more than three or four outside boards, while the latter suggests no more than two other boards. More interestingly, directors themselves have also admitted that their time and attention are dissipated by holding too many board positions. They believed that multiple directorships result in their insufficient professional responsibilities on each board. Hence, they agreed that the number of CEOs' and directors' directorships should be limited. Consequently, academics have increasingly raised their concerns and focus on both sides of the busyness of directors. Some of them suggest that reputational and busyness effects play around the agency problems within firms. This inclines researchers to construct a more insightful picture about the actions of directors, especially in the financial sector where there exists a stricter regulatory structure, high leverage, high opaqueness, and the potential for contagion. Following the essence of the ongoing controversy, the main focus of this book is to provide readers with theoretical aspects, particularly the effects of board busyness-related topics through the global banking system and differential banking models: Islamic and conventional banks.

However, I need to admit that I used to face some challenges and difficulties about theories when beginning to conduct my research. Therefore, I would like to write this book most concisely and easily for readers to follow the overview of fundamental issues. I believe that this book will become one of the most useful handbooks of future early career researchers and students who want to explore the research field about governance and particularly busyness.

In brief, this book delivers some essential concepts and theoretical perspectives of corporate governance and board busyness. It indeed explores how and why board busyness and corporate governance in the banking sector affect a set of financial outcomes including performance, risk-taking, and corporate financial policies, and discusses the market valuation of those factors. It discusses, by reviewing a comprehensive list of academic evidence, how the unique nature and characteristics of banks influence their corporate governance mechanisms, particularly board busyness function, and why board multiple directorships, once acclaimed as a new trend in the past few decades in the labor market, can become a contributing factor to banking stability in future. The book also looks at the future research directions of board busyness and concerns about the corporate governance policy including the regulatory changes of appointing directors.

This book, titled *Fundamentals of Board Busyness and Corporate Governance*, is divided into four main parts.

- Part I: The first part (Chaps. 1, 2, and 3) explains theoretical aspects related to corporate governance structures and mechanisms (i.e., agency, resource dependence, stakeholder, legitimacy, signaling, good management, slack resource, behavioral), board management and corporate governance mechanism in the banking sector, and hypotheses of board busyness as well as existing evidence in this topic.
- Part II: The second part (Chap. 4) focuses on the fundamental differences between the conventional and Islamic banking systems such as business models, corporate governance mechanisms, agency conflicts, and dividend models. I further provide some existing evidence about the comparison between these two banking models.
- Part III: The third part (Chap. 5) looks at the board busyness hypotheses for banks. It specifically discusses the theoretical associations between board busyness and the financial outcomes of banks. To review this part, I emphasize three main aspects: theoretical discussions, empirical evidence, and a relative comparison between conventional and Islamic banks. I then provide some discussions about the endogeneity problems existing in corporate governance and board busyness research and their treatments.
- Part IV: The fourth and final part (Chap. 6) suggests new directions in board busyness research, in both financial and non-financial sectors.

Newcastle Upon Tyne, UK Vu Quang Trinh

Acknowledgments

I would like to express my gratitude to Newcastle University Business School, Newcastle University, UK, where I have conducted and completed my doctoral (PhD) thesis that has then motivated me to produce this important theoretical book. Yet, the book has been rewritten in a different way from the original version of the thesis and focuses solely on theoretical aspects. I would also like to thank Rocio Torregrosa (Associate Editor, Business & Economics, Springer) and Ramya Prakash (Project Coordinator) for their continuous support and patience during the book publication process from initial stages.

I am very grateful to professors Marwa Elnahass, Aly Salama, Marwan Izzeldin, Rosie Cao, Abdullah Aljuqhaiman, Vinh Xuan Vo, Neelu Seetaram, Marco Chi Keung Lau, Thinh Pham, Teng Li, Hang Nguyen, Ngan Luong, other colleagues and friends working at Newcastle University for their valuable comments, and/or other close supports on the book and core papers used in the book. Finally, I would like to send my special thanks to my family and loved ones for their patience and support during this book project.

The views expressed in this book are the author's own and do not necessarily reflect those of the Newcastle University, UK. In addition, the book is motivated from the author's PhD dissertation, and publications in highly regarded journals including *Review of Quantitative Finance and Accounting*, *European Journal of Finance*, and *International Review of Financial Analysis*. However, all contents have been completely changed, updated, and revised.

Chapter 4, Sect. 4.3.5, is built on one of my previous publications (Sect. 2.2, Alternative dividend models) with minor revisions: Trinh V.Q., Elnahass, M., Salama, A., 2021. *Board busyness and new insights into alternative bank dividends models*. Review of Quantitative Finance and Accounting, 56 (4), 1289–1328. It is published by Springer, an open access article distributed under the terms of the Creative Commons CC BY license, which permits unrestricted use, distribution, and reproduction in any medium, provided the original work is properly cited. Link: https://link.springer.com/article/10.1007/s11156-020-00924-7#rightslink. I also cited a direct quotation on page 1 of the book, Chap. 1.

Other chapters are only motivated (but they are completely rewritten and restructured like a new piece of work) from some theoretical parts of my doctoral (PhD) thesis, *titled* "Effects of board busyness on financial stability, market valuations and dividend pay-outs: evidence from alternative banking models." Its electronic version is published in the Newcastle University e-Thesis Repository. This work is licensed under the following license: Creative Commons Attribution-Noncommercial-No Derivative Works 3.0.

Vu Quang Trinh

About This Book

This book delivers the essential concepts and theoretical perspectives of corporate governance and board busyness. It uses the unique context of a dual banking system to capture the potential effects of such aspects on corporate outcomes. Board busyness refers to a board with a substantial proportion of "busy" members who hold multiple directorships. In most cases, directors are "over-boarded," which means that they hold an excessive number of seats across different boards. The busyness of individuals is gauged to infer their monitoring and recommending abilities through their involvement, efforts, knowledge, skills, and experience, and hence, their behavior in financial contexts. Yet, an assessment of board busyness and its effects is challenging and inconclusive concerning the two opposing arguments surrounding this board attribute: reputation and busyness. The book is the first to thoroughly discuss this up-to-date concept within the dual banking system, and it is designed to help new researchers in this field and students boost their research and academic careers.

Contents

About the Author

Vu Quang Trinh is Lecturer in Accounting and Finance at Newcastle University Business School, Newcastle University, UK. Trinh is recognized as an international expert in the areas of corporate governance, board busyness, leadership, and global financial management. His recent research interests include tourism finance and governance, corporate social responsibilities, and cybersecurity risk disclosure. His publications appear in the world-leading and top-tier research journals such as *Annals of Tourism Research, European Journal of Finance, Journal of International Financial Markets, Institutions and Money, International Review of Financial Analysis, Review of Quantitative Finance and Accounting,* and *International Journal of Finance and Economics*, among several high-quality research projects. Other working papers are under reviewed (or R&R) by world-leading journals. Trinh is also the Fellow of the Higher Education Academy (HEA), the member of the European Accounting Association (EAA), British Accounting and Finance Association (BAFA), and Society for Financial Studies (SFS).

List of Abbreviations

2SLS	Two-stage least square
3SLS	Three-stage least square
AAOFI	Accounting and Auditing Organization for Islamic Financial Institutions
AGM	Annual general meeting
AMEX	American Stock Exchange
BLUE	Best linear unbiased estimators
CEO	Chief executive officer
Chair	Chairman
CLRM	Classical linear regression
COVID-19	Coronavirus 2 (SARS-CoV-2)
EBIT	Earnings before interests and taxes
GLS	Generalized least square
GMM	Two-step system generalized method of moments
IAHs	Investment account holders
IFSB	Islamic Financial Service Board
ILS	Method of indirect least squares
IVs	Instrumental variables
LUE	Linear unbiased estimators
NASDAQ	National Association of Securities Dealers Automated Quotations
NPV	Net present value
NYSE	New York Stock Exchange
OLS	Ordinary least square
PLS	Profit-loss sharing
PSIA	Profit and Loss Saving and Investment Accounts
SSB	Shari'ah Supervisory Board
SUR	Seemingly unrelated regressions
UK	United Kingdom
US	United States
VIF	Variance inflation factor

List of Abbreviations

List of Figures

List of Table

Chapter 1
Theories in Corporate Governance

> Regulators and market participants in capital markets have long emphasised on the critical role of the board of directors, as a core corporate governance mechanism, in promoting a country's economic growth and financial stability. A weak system of governance tends to offer substantial managerial opportunities to engage in risk-taking activities and fraudulent acts.[1]
>
> —Elnahass, Omoteso, Salama and Trinh (2020, Pg.201)

Corporate Governance is regarded as one of the enormous practical important subjects. It is widely mentioned and studied in a large number of research disciplines such as microeconomics, organisational economics and theory, finance, management, accounting, psychology, law, among many others. Each of these disciplines defines and views corporate governance in a dissimilar way, somewhat like a popular story about the apocryphal group of blind individuals who are trying to identify an elephant by touching each describing dissimilar parts of that elephant. Turnbull (1997) has then encompassed all those different perspectives by considering corporate governance as the influences (controllers/regulators appointments, production organisation and sale of goods and services) which can exert significant impacts on organisational processes. This general definition of corporate governance is in line with the definitions provided by prior literature. For example, according to Demb and Neubauer (1992), corporate governance is viewed as the process by which a firm can respond to the stakeholders' rights and wishes. Monks and Minow (1995) state that corporate governance is simply a relation among different parties in determining the corporate directions as well as its performance.

More importantly, Tricker (1994) claims that corporate governance can resolve some matters facing boards of directors, especially the interaction and relationship of such boards with managers, shareholders and other stakeholders (e.g., creditors, debt financiers, analysts, auditors and firm regulators) who are interested in the corporate affairs. Blair (1995) and other business school scholars and management consultants

[1] https://link.springer.com/content/pdf/10.1007/s11156-019-00841-4.pdf

V. Quang Trinh, *Fundamentals of Board Busyness and Corporate Governance*, Contributions to Management Science,
https://doi.org/10.1007/978-3-030-89228-9_1

then support this argument by asserting that the phrase corporate governance is often narrowly applied to research questions related to the structure, characteristics and functions of boards of directors. Taken together, corporate governance in this book is narrowly viewed as the structure that the management team at the institutional apex is managed and controlled by the structures of boards of directors, compensation and remuneration for executives, as well as other supervisory and bonding schemes (Donaldson 1990). In other words, this book mainly focuses on the boardroom but extends the scope to wider stakeholders of banking institutions. Such wider concerns will reflect the audience for a firm's annual reports.

Corporate governance theorists suggest four perspectives on the board roles consisting of:

(i) *Legalistic*
(ii) *Resource Dependence*
(iii) *Class Hegemony*
(iv) *Agency theory*

Under the *legalistic* perspective, the board of directors is responsible for carrying out its legally mandated duties, which may include the following:

(i) *representing shareholders' interests*
(ii) *protecting shareholders' interest*
(iii) *managing the corporation without interference in day-to-day operations*

Under the *resource dependence* perspective, the board of directors plays as a cooptative mechanism which aims at:

(i) *extracting useful (inside and outside) resources that are essential for firm outcomes*
(ii) *serving as a boundary spanning role*
(ii) *enhancing corporate legitimacy*

Under the *class hegemony* perspective, the board of directors perpetuates the power and control of the ruling capitalist elite over social and economic institutions.

Under the *agency* perspective, the board of directors monitors actions on the agents, e.g., managers, to ensure their efficiency and to protect principals' (e.g., shareholders') interests. Hence, a board of directors is regarded as a professional referee who serves as one of the monitoring agents that has a legal and moral obligation in aligning manager and shareholder interests to ensure that businesses are run in the best interests of shareholders.

When evaluating the effects of board characteristics on organisational outcomes, scholars often employ *either* a single perspective above (i.e., legalistic, resource dependence, class hegemony and (iv) agency) *or* combine them into an integrative theoretical model. The full integrative model includes three vital functions as follows:

(i) *To identify the conditional nature of associations among board attributes and roles and corporate outcomes depending on internal and external circumstantial contingencies.*
(ii) *To propose a specific arrangement of associations among factors that presents a means of combined various study streams.*
(iii) *To identify the multidimensional nature of corporate outcomes.*

Four important attributes (i.e., Composition; Characteristics; Structure; and Process) of the board of directors could be then identified in such an integrative model of roles. They should be highly interrelated but not necessarily exhaustive. Each board attribute encompasses relevant elements that are expected to contribute indirectly, through board role, to corporate outcomes (see Hillman et al. 2000, 2009; Pfeffer and Salancik 1978). Board composition includes *board size, types of directors, minority, etc.* Board characteristics comprise *directors' background, directors' personality*, etc. Board structure reflects *the number of committees' types, committee membership, the flow of information among those committees, board leadership, patterns of committee membership*. And finally, the boarding process refers to *frequency and length of meetings, CEO-board interface, level of consensus among directors on issues at hand, the extent to which the board is involved in evaluating itself*. These main board attributes should have a temporal linkage in the model as below:

- *Board composition influences characteristics of directors.*
- *Board characteristics influences board structure.*
- *Board structure then shape board internal process.*

The board's influences on the corporate decision-making, its risks and performance, value and financial policies could, arguably, take place directly and indirectly. The direct impacts of the boards occur through the relationship between the four board attributes above and corporate outcomes. The indirect impacts of the board, meanwhile, are reflected through the influences of board attributes on three role performances of the board (i.e., service, strategy and control), in turn, impact on firm outcomes. Specifically, the functions of the boards of directors are expressed, in a complementary fashion, through:

(i) the control role, as informed by *agency* theory
(ii) the strategy role, as informed by *resource dependence* theory
(ii) the service role, as informed by *resource dependence* theory

Therefore, the influences of the board multi-directorships (i.e., board busyness) are assessed underneath two perspectives.

- On the one hand, boards with "busy" directors are likely to have more links with different sectors of the external environment, ensuring essential resources for the firm which may improve its service role. This is consistent with resource dependence theory.
- On the other hand, holding too many additional positions can mitigate the control ability of the boards, by reducing their monitoring and evaluating managers and firm performance. This is in line with agency theory.

Before taking a step forward to discuss board busyness effects as well as in-depth knowledge about the dual banking system (Islamic versus Conventional banks), this chapter will provide readers some fundamental knowledge of popular theories in the corporate governance field as follows:

1. *Agency theory*
2. *Resource dependence theory*
3. *Stakeholder theory*
4. *Legitimacy theory*
5. *Information signalling theory*
6. *Good management and slack resource theory*
7. *A brief of behavioural finance theories*

1.1 Agency Theory

Under the simple financial perspective, the vital matter in corporate governance is to construct rules (e.g., guidelines, directions) and incentives (e.g., implicit or explicit "*contracts*") to effectively align the behaviours of management/executives (agents) with the wishes of owners (principals). The problem of agents can occur when they opportunistically act and make decisions based on their self-benefit but not the interests of the principals (Hawley and Williams 1996). Following previous studies, this book addresses this problem as agency conflicts with a sum of agency costs of (i) *monitoring management* (the agent), (ii) *bonding the agent to the principals*, and (iii) *residual losses*.

Among these three main agency costs, the last one (i.e., residual losses) is considered as the key feature because the other two expenditures (i.e., *monitoring* expenditures and *bonding* expenditures) are suffered only in the degree to which they produce cost-effective decreases in the residual loss. The residual loss refers to a fall in the corporate value obtained when entrepreneurs dilute their ownerships leading to the shift out of income and into managerial expenditure, and in turn, this loss. Monitoring and bonding costs can help restore the firm performance toward the pre-dilution stages. The minimum sum of those three factors, therefore, will be the irreducible agency costs (Williamson 1988). Equity purchasers will only pay for the projected performance of a firm after taking into consideration agency costs of these three kinds (Jensen and Meckling 1976).

The agency problem has been considered as one of the most crucial elements of the so-called contractual view of the corporation (Coase 1937; Jensen and Meckling 1976; Fama and Jensen 1983a, 1983b). The essence of this problem is the separation of ownership and control, or—in easier understanding terminology, of management and finance. A corporate manager can raise funds for his/her firm from capital providers (i.e., investors) either to put them to effective use or to cash out his/her holdings in the company. The capital providers need the ability of the managers to generate returns on their money while the managers need the capital from these

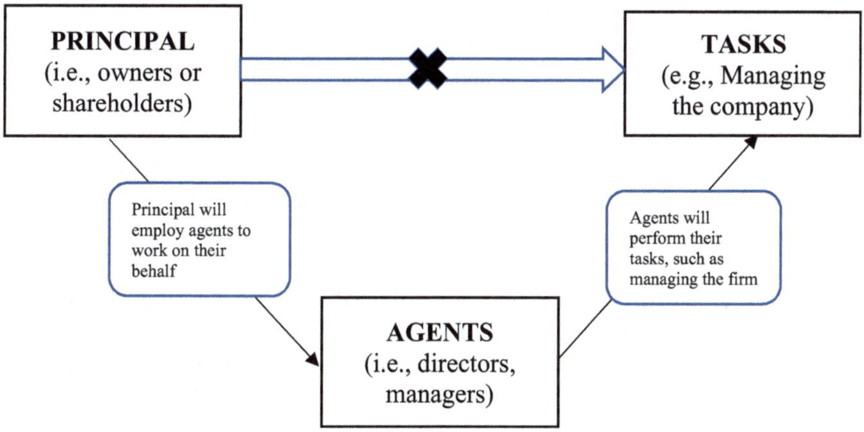

Fig. 1.1 Agency theory. *Source:* author (based on Jensen and Meckling 1976)

providers to invest or cash out their holdings. However, the funds of the providers probably become a worthless piece of paperback from the manager. Thus, in this context, the difficulties capital providers have in assuring that their capital will not be expropriated or wasted on negative net present value investments refer to the agency problem.

The fundamental inference of agency theory is that a firm's value may not be maximised as desired by principals since management possesses discrepancies that can allow them to expropriate value to themselves before the firm owners. In an ideal world, owners of the firm can require managers to sign a complete and legal contract which specifies exactly and thoroughly what and how those managers would do under all states of the world and most importantly, how profits could be distributed to the owners and other stockholders. In practice, a massive problem is that it is too difficult to describe and foresee future contingencies, technologically leading to an incomplete contract. As such, managers can obtain the right to make personal decisions that cannot be clarified or anticipated in the legal contract under which debt or equity is contributed (Shleifer and Vishny 1997; Grossman and Hart 1986; Hart and Moore 2007; Downs 1957). This results in the principals' problem (Ross 1973) and agency problem (Fama and Jensen 1983b). See Fig. 1.1 below.

In addition, in the cases a firm's funding is collected from a large number of investors, these investors themselves are often holding a very small portion of the whole fund; and for this reason, they are very poorly informed to work out even the control rights they should have. The free-rider problem discourages those individual investors to learn about the firms they own, or even take part in the governance, just like citizens are not paid to get informed regarding the political candidates as well as a vote (Shleifer and Vishny 1997). Consequently, if courts or capital providers actively get involved in detailed contract enforcement, the managers' effective control rights, and thus, the boardroom they have for discretionary distribution of capital, would end up being much more extensive than they should have been.

From the above background of agency theory in early studies, the subsequent research stream in corporate governance normally discusses the agency conflicts or agency costs in cases that complete and contingent contracts between managers and investors are infeasible. The agency theory formula to principal-agent conflict looks to boards of directors to supervise the verification process on behalf of principals. The boards of directors accommodate inside and affiliated members, including senior managers, as well as outside directors. On the one hand, insiders have unique business knowledge which outsiders do not have (i.e., information asymmetry), provide valuable information about the institution's activities, but are influenced by CEO power. Boards have the fiduciary responsibility of monitoring the actions of executives (agents) to protect shareholders' interests (principals). Therefore, monitoring by the boards is essential since potential agency costs could be incurred when executives pursue their self-interest at the expense of shareholders' and other stakeholders' interests.

The uniqueness of the agency relationships at institutions offering financial services, whether Islamic or conventional, stems from the agents' duty to protect and promote the interests of all capital providers, including depositors, investors and shareholders.

1.2 Resource Dependence Theory

Almost four decades have passed since resource dependence theory was introduced by a seminar work of Pfeffer and Salancik (1978). Over time, this theory has been applied broadly across various research areas to explain how a firm could reduce environmental interdependence and uncertainty. Up to date, it is still one of the most influential theories in organisational theory and strategic management. This theory starts from the premise that organisation is an *open system*, dependent on contingencies and external resources in their environment (i.e., includes all structures, actors and events that affect the dependence of an organisation on outside resources) to operate and survive.

Resource dependence theory focuses on the role of directors serving on the boards in providing access to corporate resources and securing these resources to a firm through their linkages to the markets and external environment. It concentrates on the appointment of representatives of independent institutions as an effective means for increasing access to essential resources critical to corporate success. For instance, an outside director who is also working in a law company can provide his/her legal advice in the periodic board meetings or even private communication with management or executive boards that should otherwise be more expensive for an organisation to secure (Pfeffer and Salancik 1978; Biermann and Harsch 2017; Hatch 1997; Hillman et al. 2009; Johnson et al. 1996).

The theory implies that members of a board (e.g., directors, managers) can bring useful resources (e.g., information, skills, legitimacy, and networking) to all the

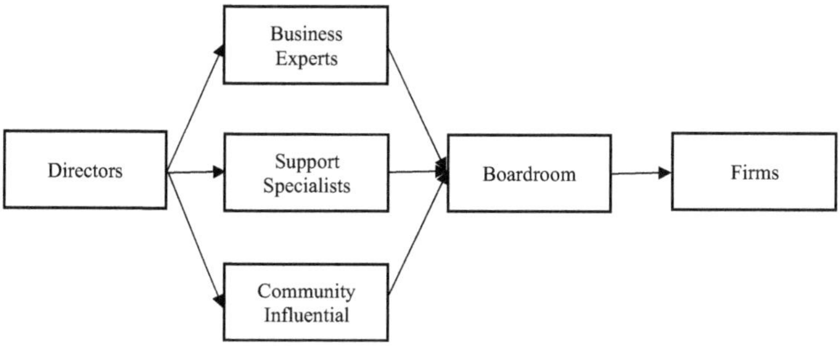

Fig. 1.2 Different types of resources. *Source:* author (based on Jensen and Meckling 1976)

firms where they are serving. Indeed, strong support has accrued for *four* main benefits of those directors as follows:

(i) *essential information by providing some advice and counsel.*
(ii) *accessing to information channels between the organisations and environmental contingencies.*
(iii) *providing preferential access to corporate resources.*
(iv) *Providing legitimacy.*

The dynamic nature of the boards; e.g., altering board composition when environmental needs change, is likely to be a nearly normative convention. Firms can attract and recruit powerful communities influential onto their boards. High-regulated firms like banks tend to need more outsiders with relevant industry knowledge and experience. Those outsiders can enhance corporate social performance.

In theory, there are *three* main types of directors corresponding to the different types of resources those directors can bring to a board (Hillman et al. 2000; Pfeffer and Salancik 1978; Provan 1980; Goodstein and Polasky 1999): (Fig. 1.2)

- *Business experts:* could be the current and former senior executives and directors of other for-profit companies, can provide their expertise and experience on business strategy, decision-making and problem solving.
- *Support specialists:* could be the lawyers, bankers, representatives for insurance companies, and public relations experts, they can support for the firm in their specialised field.
- *Community influential:* could be political leaders, university faculty, members of clergy and leaders of social and community institutions.

Despite the predominant theory in the studies on the boards is agency theory, the greatest research influence in this area might be resource dependence. Corporate boards allow companies to minimise dependence or increase resources. Previous literature on the boards highlights that resource dependence theory provides a more successful lens for understanding boards than any other board perspective including agency theory. Resource dependence scholars stress two board attributes (i.e.,

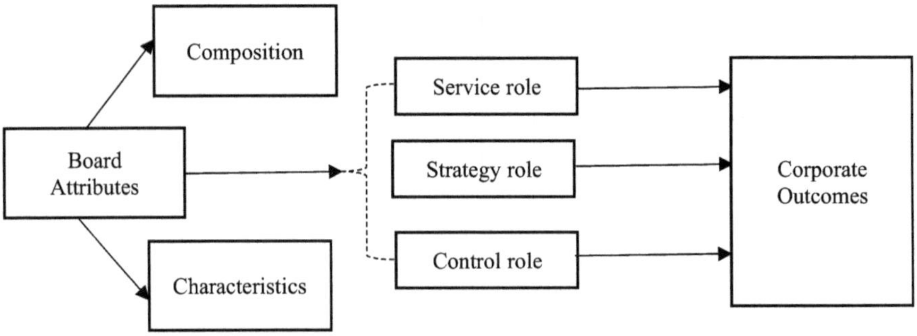

Fig. 1.3 Resource dependence theory. *Source:* Author (based on Zahra and Pearce 1989)

composition and characteristics) as antecedents of three board roles (i.e., service, strategy and control). They suggest that directors of the board can bring good resources for successful firm operations because of their professions and communities, hence, enhance the legitimacy in the society of the firm and accomplish goals of efficiency and better performance. For instance, those directors can be actively involved in the strategic arena through advice and guidance to the firm's CEO, by introducing their own evaluates or alternatives. Thus, directors can shape these creativities directly by recommending new business ideas or introducing their analyses. However, developing and executing those strategies are tasks of CEOs (Johnson et al. 1996; Zahra and Pearce 1989; Dalton et al. 2007; Pfeffer 1972) (Fig. 1.3).

Early empirical evidence on this theory focuses on board size and board composition which serve as board ability indicators providing critical resources to the organisation. Pfeffer (1972) explores that size of the boards is likely to be associated with the corporate environment needs and those with higher interdependence require a greater ratio of independent/outside directors. Sanders and Carpenter (1998) also support this by providing evidence on the positive link between board size and a firm's level of internationalisation. Other scholars then have emphasised the high need to "match" resources brought by the boards with the corporate needs (Hillman et al. 2009). Boyd (1990) contends that board size is a hindrance, whereas board interlocks or multiple directorships are a benefit, implying that "resource-rich" directors should be the concentration of board composition. Therefore, it is important to take into account not only the number but also the types of directors serving in the boardroom (Hillman et al. 2009).

1.3 Stakeholder Theory

Stakeholder theory claims a broader concept of corporate governance that is applied in modern businesses (see Haridan et al. 2018). In general terms, it could be considered as an extended form of agency theory. While agency theory focuses on the conflicts of interests between managers and shareholders, stakeholder theory extends these conflicts to the case of a broad range of stakeholders. More specifically, stakeholder theory emphasises that the decision-making of managers and the interests of all stakeholders have intrinsic value; no one set of interests is expected to dominate the others (Freeman et al. 2018).

The theory could be well-reflected through the unique roles of boards within banking institutions in balancing the different interests of several stakeholders. In other words, it provides greater latitude in widening the concept of corporate governance as managers and directors need to serve both the interests of the bank owners and the interests of other stakeholders such as regulators, policymakers, local communities, creditors, customers, employees, investors and market participants (Garcia-Torea et al. 2016). Given that, unlike non-financial firms, banks themselves should be thought of as groupings of stakeholders, managing their interests, needs and viewpoints might be the main purpose of banking institutions. This management of stakeholders' interests is the duty of bank managers, who are expected to control their business for the stakeholders' benefit. This ensures their rights and participation in the bank's decision-making process (Elyasiani and Zhang 2015). These managers should also act as the agents of the stakeholders to guarantee the bank's survival and hence ensure the long-run stakes of each interest group.

Existing research has found a significant role in effective corporate governance practices, but this depends on how well a firm can manage the diverse expectations and interests of various groups of stakeholders. Nevertheless, building a good model to devise a principle for making trade-offs among diverse stakeholders appears to be challenging.

1.4 Legitimacy Theory

Legitimacy theory also claims a broader concept of corporate governance that is applied in modern businesses. In general terms, it could be considered as an extended form of resource dependence theory. While resource dependence theory discourses the role of directors in offering valuable resources to their firms such as knowledge and expertise, networking, experience and skills, the legitimacy may influence resource dependence theory as well as other institutional theories because it could be related to the reputational gain of an organisation through legitimacy.

The term '*legitimacy*' refers to a generalized perception that shows the desirable, proper, or appropriate actions made by an entity in the context of a socially constructed system of norms, values, beliefs, and definitions. Based on this concept, legitimacy theory has become one of the most popular theoretical constructs used for making viable predictions. It plays a vital role in describing the behaviours of firms when they implement and improve the voluntary disclosures of social, economic and environmental information. This development of disclosure aims to fulfil the corporate social contract, which helps to recognise firms' goals and their survival in a turbulent environment (Idowu et al. 2013). Vitally, the activities of organisations should be following the expectations of society regarding social and moral values. They need to justify their existence through legitimate economic and social actions that will not endanger the existence of society and the natural environment. If they do not, they will be severely sanctioned by the society in which they operate, leading to their possible failure (Burlea and Popa 2013).

Furthermore, legitimacy theory is observed as an *anchor point* of a vastly expanded theoretical apparatus that solves the normative and cognitive forces (i.e., those are related to the constraint, construct, and empower institutional actors) (see Suchman 1995). As such, corporate managers have earned the firm's reputation by formulating different strategies to maintain the legitimacy of the firm's operations, thus enhancing the corporate stakeholders' confidence (Patten 1992). One can translate this theory into the way that firms commit themselves to adopt organisational social behaviour in their corporate governance mechanism to ensure compliance with the values and social norms of the respective societies that they operate in (Golant and Sillince 2007). This argument implies that the integrity of a firm might be undermined when the activities of that organisation show less legitimate social behaviour (Dowling and Pfeffer 1975). Also, a firm's legitimacy and reputation could represent assessments of a corporation by a social system (Deephouse and Carter 2005).

However, the quality of the legitimacy appears to depend a great deal on the bank's management team, which has a central role in assuring the interaction between the internal and external environment and in stopping, in time, the destruction of the bank's image. In that way, firm managers and the management of legitimacy should be interconnected, as they critically affect one another to fulfil the main objectives of economy, society and environment (Idowu et al. 2013). Accordingly, the sustainability of this theory rests upon the management's heritage, which links the conventional social norms and values to modern ethics.

1.5 Information Signalling Theory

Strategic management research has recently viewed information signalling theory as an increasingly popular theoretical framework that directs attention to central issues facing strategic decision-makers (Bergh and Gibbons 2011; Connelly et al. 2011). The issues are how these decision-makers can employ signals to mitigate the uncertainty related to the selection of a choice set in cases that have incomplete and asymmetrically distributed information (Spence 1973, 1974, 2002). For instance, a change in corporate name (Lee 2001) could be shrouded in imperfect information and generate uncertain prospects for corporate stockholders. Those stockholders may respond to this by seeking out signals (which are considered by Bergh et al. (2014) and Spence (1974) as the observable actions providing information associated with unobservable attributes as well as likely outcomes) that can help close the gap between what stakeholders know about the company and what these stakeholders wish to know (Miller and del Carmen Triana 2009; Bergh et al. 2014).

To clarify how related parties can address information problems, other perspectives, i.e., strategic sense-making (Gioia and Chittipeddi 1991) and information processing theory (Galbraith 1973) assert that stockholders search for some corporate clues, interpret them and are directed by their understandings when formulating their actions. Signalling theory, with a distinctive feature of "separating equilibrium", proposes a supplementary and imperative step by stipulating how signal senders (e.g., firms) and observers (e.g., stockholders) can distinguish between (or "separate") high and low-quality actors upon on an observable signal (Bergh et al. 2014).

In the strategic management and corporate governance context, researchers are concerned with the signals related to corporate governance that a firm sends to the market. Indeed, signalling theory (Bergh and Gibbons 2011; Connelly et al. 2011; Bergh et al. 2014) argues that firms can enhance the investors' trust if they can expose good corporate governance information to the market which eliminates the information asymmetry between firm managers and investors. Prior studies show that investors make their investment decisions relying on the information sent out from the firm (Poitevin 1990; Ravid and Sarig 1991). Under a transactional setting, when an investor is considering purchasing stock from a listed firm, this firm might be interested in signalling the hidden value of the equity investment by undervaluing the equity (Allen and Faulhaber 1989) or providing that investor information related to the boards of directors and management that enhances the credibility of its strategy (Higgins and Gulati 2006).

This theory makes several conditions:

(i) An indirect interdependence between firms (signal sender) and investors (signal receiver) (Scitovsky 1954).
(ii) Uncertainty about the true nature of the firm before releasing the signal (Spence 1973).
(iii) Unbounded rational agent such that the firm is anticipated to take action to maximise its profits, and the investor is posited to understand the signal released by the firm (March 1978).
(iv) A moral hazard constraint such that the investor cannot change any conditions during the period between the signal release and the pay-off withdrawal.

Under these assumptions of the theory, holding information content constant, firm valuations of investors may depend on how transactions are categorised and presented (Peng and Xiong 2006). The extent of disclosure, reporting transparency and news outcomes, which highlight favourable aspects of the set of available public information, imply stock overvaluing, and thereby positive subsequent firm valuations. By contrast, outcomes that highlight negative aspects suggest stock underpricing.

Given the opposing effects of "busy" boards of directors (i.e., those holding multiple directorships) on the board quality (see details in Chap. 3), signalling theorists can predict that board multiple directorships are (1) higher-priced if they successfully signal better governance to investors, and otherwise (2) lower or not valued. If the (1) is the case, when firms increase the proportion of "busy" directors, they communicate to the market that the board monitoring ability to managers increases that meet the investors' interests (Connelly et al. 2011) which boosts stock value.

Whether outside directors are highly certified, via their multiple directorships, is a signal that creates a "separating equilibrium" for all parties involved. To the extent that receivers (stock market or investors) and signaller (firms or directors) are rational, in the first scenario, "busy" directors will become certified as high-quality monitors and "non-busy" directors will not. Noting that the quality of directors is more about the unobservable ability of the firm to earn future positive free cash flow. "Busy" directors are thereby likely to become high-quality monitors if they create a higher performance than "non-busy" directors.

From investors' perspective, the number of directorships held by directors thus may separate high-quality directors from low-quality directors. Equilibrium is achieved if the signal is confirmed by the high performance of directors fulfilling the firm's post-hiring expectations. More broadly, "separating equilibrium" might occur if investors and firms weigh the returns and costs of investing in a busyness signal and make optimising decisions regarding such signal; both senders (the firms) and receivers (the investors) have beliefs about the association between the signal and the unobservable attributes of the signaller, and post-signal data and experience confirm, or disconfirm, the expectations of both the firm and the investors (see Bergh et al. 2014). The second scenario is the opposite case.

1.6 Good Management and Slack Resource Theory

Good management theory can be used to explain the relationship between corporate governance, cost of capital and firm valuation (Pae and Choi 2011). This theory reflects firm value implications through the positive linkage between the high quality of corporate governance, better management and provision of high-quality information, which mitigates agency problems and firm-specific risks, as well as promotes both ethical commitment and corporate social responsibility (Neville et al. 2005; Money and Schepers 2007; Jamali et al. 2008). This results in the enhancement of market reputation (Neville et al. 2005) and the value relevance of good corporate governance.

However, in an efficient market, all value-relevant information is instantaneously incorporated in the equity value (Choi and Jung 2008; Preston and O'bannon 1997). Nevertheless, it might take time for the firm earnings to reflect the benefits of good corporate governance. Therefore, better corporate governance implies an increased long-term financial performance which yields a higher stock price as investors often use future performance to establish their required rate of return or cost of capital. It is anticipated that the required rate of return is lower for firms with strong corporate governance than for firms with weak corporate governance.

Research could predict a similar relationship between a "busy" board of directors and the required rate of return if such board busyness brings the reputation benefits (see details in Chap. 3): the required rate of return is lower for firms with "busy" boards and hence, higher firm valuation. Otherwise, if reputation benefits are dominated by the busyness effect, the lower monitoring quality of the boards is likely to be correlated with the higher firm's cost of equity capital and the lower level of corporate ethical commitment.

Slack resource theory further demonstrates that firms with higher market valuations tend to have more slack economic resources to invest in the improvement of the corporate governance mechanism and board quality. They are more likely to make ethical business decisions, which in turn results in appreciation by ethically conscious investors and therefore leads to even much higher firm valuation, creating a virtuous circle (Pae and Choi 2011). However, entrenched managers may have incentives to divert slack resources or free cash flows for their private interests (e.g., building an empire, increasing their compensation) (Jensen 1986). In such a case, those managers are less likely to use slack resources to invest in social performance domains and improve corporate governance. Therefore, monitoring the effectiveness of the board of directors towards those managers becomes more indispensable and the research in this area, hence, can expect a link between such monitoring ability (*via* "busyness" of boards) and the accountabilities of managers, then the firm value. Yet the monitoring ability of a "busy" board depends on the agency problems and the complexities of the institutional environment.

1.7 Behavioural Finance Theories

Behavioural finance theories such as the representativeness heuristic, suggest that individuals are likely to overestimate the likelihood that an event, which is related to the similarity between the properties of such event and the parent population, occurs (Chan et al. 2004). For a firm having a high reputable director who is recruited by several firms (i.e., "busy" directors), investors may overestimate the probability that he/she is a better monitor since they overuse the similarity on looks and under-use the fact that a "busy" director certified as a better monitor may constitute only a small percentage of the population (e.g., low rate). Representativeness bias, therefore, typically results in the initial overvaluing of investors and may anticipate subsequent return reversals. By contrast, conservatism bias predicts that investors update their beliefs slowly (Edwards 1968). They may over-use the base rate and under-use the representativeness of the evidence. This may lead to investors' under-reaction regarding the information received.

Furthermore, theories about the limited attention and processing power of investors argue that informationally equivalent disclosures may consume various impacts on the investors' perceptions depending on the presentation which is an immediate but far-reaching consequence of limited attention. Indeed, investors often have limited attention to information published. If such information is released in a more salient way (only implicit in the public information set), the processed form could be absorbed more easily (Hirshleifer and Teoh 2003). For example, investors are likely to ignore relevant aspects of the economic environments which they may face. This may lead inattentive investors to lose their money by neglecting such aspects, but it is reasonable if time and attention are costly.

With the assumption that investors tend to be risk-averse, highly attentive investors might encounter some obstacles related to the extent to which they are willing to take their risks to exploit mispricing. Also, limited information processing capacity tends to induce investors to use information in the form it is displayed with lower costs of processing information, rather than modifying it appropriately; but this may induce errors such as functional fixation.

Although researchers can expect a significant connection between "busy" boards of directors and firm value, this relationship may be affected by the limited attention and processing power of investors (e.g., becomes insignificant). Specifically, inattentive investors may fail to take into account board "busyness" information presented in the raw form in the proxy statements as firms tend to exploit investor perceptions differently. In some cases, investors may neglect board "busyness" information if they can process more relevant information to their desire.

References

Allen, F., and G.R. Faulhaber. 1989. Signalling by underpricing in the IPO market. *Journal of Financial Economics* 23 (2): 303–323.

Bergh, D.D., and P. Gibbons. 2011. The stock market reaction to the hiring of management consultants: A signalling theory approach. *Journal of Management Studies* 48 (3): 544–567.

Bergh, D.D., B.L. Connelly, D.J. Ketchen Jr., and L.M. Shannon. 2014. Signalling theory and equilibrium in strategic management research: An assessment and a research agenda. *Journal of Management Studies* 51 (8): 1334–1360.

Biermann, R., and M. Harsch. 2017. Resource dependence theory. In *Palgrave Handbook of Inter-Organizational Relations in World Politics*, 135–155. London: Palgrave Macmillan.

Blair, M.M. 1995. Rethinking assumptions behind corporate governance. *Challenge* 38 (6): 12–17.

Boyd, B. 1990. Corporate linkages and organizational environment: A test of the resource dependence model. *Strategic Management Journal* 11 (6): 419–430.

Burlea, A.S., and I. Popa. 2013. Legitimacy theory in encyclopedia of corporate social responsibility, 1579–1584.

Chan, W.S., R. Frankel, and S.P. Kothari. 2004. Testing behavioral finance theories using trends and consistency in financial performance. *Journal of Accounting and Economics* 38: 3–50.

Choi, T.H., and J. Jung. 2008. Ethical commitment, financial performance, and valuation: An empirical investigation of Korean companies. *Journal of Business Ethics* 81 (2): 447–463.

Coase, R.H. 1937. The nature of the firm. *Economica* 4 (16): 386–405.

Connelly, B.L., S.T. Certo, R.D. Ireland, and C.R. Reutzel. 2011. Signaling theory: A review and assessment. *Journal of Management* 37 (1): 39–67.

Dalton, D.R., M.A. Hitt, S.T. Certo, and C.M. Dalton. 2007. The fundamental agency problem and its mitigation. *Academy of Management Annals* 1 (1): 1–64.

Deephouse, D.L., and S.M. Carter. 2005. An examination of differences between organizational legitimacy and organizational reputation. *Journal of Management Studies* 42 (2): 329–360.

Demb, A., and F.F. Neubauer. 1992. The corporate board: Confronting the paradoxes. *Long Range Planning* 25 (3): 9–20.

Donaldson, L. 1990. The ethereal hand: Organizational economics and management theory. *Academy of Management Review* 15 (3): 369–381.

Dowling, J., and J. Pfeffer. 1975. Organizational legitimacy: Social values and organizational behavior. *Pacific Sociological Review* 18 (1): 122–136.

Downs, A. 1957. An economic theory of political action in a democracy. *Journal of Political Economy* 65 (2): 135–150.

Edwards, W. 1968. Conservatism in human information processing. Formal representation of human judgment.

Elyasiani, E., and L. Zhang. 2015. Bank holding company performance, risk, and "busy" board of directors. *Journal of Banking & Finance* 60: 239–251.

Fama, E.F., and M.C. Jensen. 1983a. Separation of ownership and control. *The Journal of Law and Economics* 26 (2): 301–325.

———. 1983b. Agency problems and residual claims. *The Journal of Law and Economics* 26 (2): 327–349.

Freeman, R., J. Harrison, and S. Zyglidopoulos. 2018. *Stakeholder theory: Concepts and strategies (elements in organization theory)*. Cambridge: Cambridge University Press.

Galbraith, J. 1973. *Designing complex organizations*. Reading, MA.

Garcia-Torea, N., B. Fernandez-Feijoo, and M. de la Cuesta. 2016. Board of director's effectiveness and the stakeholder perspective of corporate governance: Do effective boards promote the interests of shareholders and stakeholders? *BRQ Business Research Quarterly* 19 (4): 246–260.

Gioia, D.A., and K. Chittipeddi. 1991. Sensemaking and sensegiving in strategic change initiation. *Strategic Management Journal* 12 (6): 433–448.

Golant, B.D., and J.A. Sillince. 2007. The constitution of organizational legitimacy: A narrative perspective. *Organization Studies* 28 (8): 1149–1167.

Goodstein, E.S., and S. Polasky. 1999. *Economics and the environment*. Upper Saddle River, NJ: Prentice Hall.

Grossman, S.J., and O.D. Hart. 1986. The costs and benefits of ownership: A theory of vertical and lateral integration. *Journal of Political Economy* 94 (4): 691–719.

Haridan, N.M., A.F. Hassan, and Y. Karbhari. 2018. Governance, religious assurance and Islamic banks: Do Shariah boards effectively serve? *Journal of Management and Governance* 22 (4): 1015–1043.

Hart, O., and J. Moore. 2007. Incomplete contracts and ownership: Some new thoughts. *American Economic Review* 97 (2): 182–186.

Hatch, M.J. 1997. Irony and the social construction of contradiction in the humor of a management team. *Organization Science* 8 (3): 275–288.

Hawley, J.P., and A.T. Williams. 1996. Corporate governance in the United States: The rise of fiduciary capitalism. *School of Economics and Business Administration*.

Higgins, M.C., and R. Gulati. 2006. Stacking the deck: The effects of top management backgrounds on investor decisions. *Strategic Management Journal* 27 (1): 1–25.

Hillman, A.J., A.A. Cannella, and R.L. Paetzold. 2000. The resource dependence role of corporate directors: Strategic adaptation of board composition in response to environmental change. *Journal of Management Studies* 37 (2): 235–256.

Hillman, A.J., M.C. Withers, and B.J. Collins. 2009. Resource dependence theory: A review. *Journal of management* 35 (6): 1404–1427.

Hirshleifer, D., and S.H. Teoh. 2003. Limited attention, information disclosure, and financial reporting. *Journal of Accounting and Economics* 36 (1–3): 337–386.

Idowu, S.O., N. Capaldi, L. Zu, and A.D. Gupta. 2013. *Encyclopedia of corporate social responsibility*. Vol. 21. New York: Springer.

Jamali, D., A.M. Safieddine, and M. Rabbath. 2008. Corporate governance and corporate social responsibility synergies and interrelationships. *Corporate Governance: An International Review* 16 (5): 443–459.

Jensen, M.C. 1986. Agency costs of free cash flow, corporate finance, and takeovers. *The American Economic Review* 76 (2): 323–329.

Jensen, M.C., and W.H. Meckling. 1976. Theory of the firm: Managerial behavior, agency costs and ownership structure. *Journal of Financial Economics* 3 (4): 305–360.
Johnson, J.L., C.M. Daily, and A.E. Ellstrand. 1996. Boards of directors: A review and research agenda. *Journal of Management* 22 (3): 409–438.
Lee, P.M. 2001. What's in a name.com?: The effects of '.com' name changes on stock prices and trading activity. *Strategic Management Journal* 22 (8): 793–804.
March, J.G. 1978. Bounded rationality, ambiguity, and the engineering of choice. *The Bell Journal of Economics*, pp. 587–608.
Miller, T., and M. del Carmen Triana. 2009. Demographic diversity in the boardroom: Mediators of the board diversity–firm performance relationship. *Journal of Management Studies* 46 (5): 755–786.
Money, K., and H. Schepers. 2007. Are CSR and corporate governance converging?: A view from boardroom directors and company secretaries in FTSE100 companies in the UK. *Journal of General Management* 33 (2): 1–11.
Monks, R.A.G., and N. Minow. 1995. Corporate governance on equity ownership and corporate value. *Journal of Financial Economics* 20 (3): 293–315.
Neville, B.A., S.J. Bell, and B. Mengüç. 2005. Corporate reputation, stakeholders and the social performance-financial performance relationship. *European Journal of Marketing*.
Pae, J., and T.H. Choi. 2011. Corporate governance, commitment to business ethics, and firm valuation: Evidence from the Korean stock market. *Journal of Business Ethics* 100 (2): 323–348.
Patten, D.M. 1992. Intra-industry environmental disclosures in response to the Alaskan oil spill: A note on legitimacy theory. *Accounting, Organizations and Society* 17 (5): 471–475.
Peng, L., and W. Xiong. 2006. Investor attention, overconfidence and category learning. *Journal of Financial Economics* 80 (3): 563–602.
Pfeffer, J. 1972. Size and composition of corporate boards of directors: The organization and its environment. *Administrative Science Quarterly*, pp. 218–228.
Pfeffer, J., and G.R. Salancik. 1978. *The external control of organisations: A resource dependence perspective*. New York: Harper & Row.
Poitevin, M. 1990. Strategic financial signalling. *International Journal of Industrial Organization* 8 (4): 499–518.
Preston, L.E., and D.P. O'bannon. 1997. The corporate social-financial performance relationship: A typology and analysis. *Business & Society* 36 (4): 419–429.
Provan, K.G. 1980. Board power and organizational effectiveness among human service agencies. *Academy of Management Journal* 23 (2): 221–236.
Ravid, S.A., and O.H. Sarig. 1991. Financial signalling by committing to cash outflows. *Journal of Financial and Quantitative Analysis* 26 (2): 165–180.
Ross, S.A. 1973. The economic theory of agency: The principal's problem. *The American Economic Review* 63 (2): 134–139.
Sanders, W.G., and M.A. Carpenter. 1998. Internationalization and firm governance: The roles of CEO compensation, top team composition, and board structure. *Academy of Management Journal* 41 (2): 158–178.
Scitovsky, T. 1954. Two concepts of external economies. *Journal of Political Economy* 62 (2): 143–151.
Shleifer, A., and R.W. Vishny. 1997. A survey of corporate governance. *The Journal of Finance* 52 (2): 737–783.
Spence, A.M. 1973. Time and communication in economic and social interaction. *The Quarterly Journal of Economics* 87 (4): 651–660.
Spence, M. 1974. Competitive and optimal responses to signals: An analysis of efficiency and distribution. *Journal of Economic Theory* 7 (3): 296–332.
———. 2002. Signaling in retrospect and the informational structure of markets. *American Economic Review* 92 (3): 434–459.

Suchman, M. 1995. Managing legitimacy: Strategic and institutional approaches. *Academy of Management Review* 20 (3): 571–610.

Tricker, R.I. 1994. *International corporate governance: Text, readings, and cases*. Prentice Hall.

Turnbull, S. 1997. Corporate governance: Its scope, concerns and theories. *Corporate Governance: An International Review* 5 (4): 180–205.

Williamson, O.E. 1988. Corporate finance and corporate governance. *The Journal of Finance* 43 (3): 567–591.

Zahra, S.A., and J.A. Pearce II. 1989. Boards of directors and corporate financial performance: A review and integrative model. *Journal of Management* 15 (2): 291–334.

Chapter 2
Corporate Governance in Banking

2.1 The Importance of Governance in Banking

The Banking Sector has been through significant topsy-turvy over the past ten years, surviving a severe financial turmoil and unparalleled regulatory reform (O'Donnell and Rodda 2015). Several spectators attribute this to failures in corporate governance including lax board oversight practice which encourages excessive risk-taking and lending (Erkens et al. 2012; Kirkpatrick 2009; Sharfman 2009; Körner 2017). John et al. (1991) noticed that both, risk-adjusted deposit insurance premiums and risk-adjusted capital requirements, fail to reduce the moral hazard problem of banks as well as to fully manage their risk-taking activities. In such context, the opportunistic behaviour of management is likely to depend on corporate governance structure (Mollah et al. 2017).

Therefore, governance effectiveness of banking institutions has become an imperative subject that needs to be given a further special concern at global level, especially after the Enron debacle and the Global Crossing Bankruptcy which significantly affects the financial stability of banks worldwide (see Sierra et al. 2006; Andres and Vallelado 2008; Adams and Mehran 2012; Aebi et al. 2012; Pathan and Faff 2013; Mollah and Zaman 2015; De Haan and Vlahu 2016). Particularly, the lack of the accountability and weak performance of the boards of directors leading to their "home" bank' high risk profile, in addition to their attitude towards financial stability, market value, financial policies and ethical principles of banks, has come under increased monitoring (Mollah and Zaman 2015). The trend in this matter is to take up additional directorships of directors causing their over-boarded and being unable to fulfil their fiduciary duties, hence, might affect their supervisory performance (Elyasiani and Zhang 2015).

Focusing on banks in this book is for a number of other reasons. Foremost, banks today are likely to be highly interconnected. This is simply because of the globalisation, technological developments and new polices of financial liberalisation that

V. Quang Trinh, *Fundamentals of Board Busyness and Corporate Governance*, Contributions to Management Science,
https://doi.org/10.1007/978-3-030-89228-9_2

unsurprisingly may trigger greater risks to the financial services industry. In this regard, The Basel Committee on Banking Supervision Enhancing corporate governance for banking organisations (Emmenegger 2006) points out that it is particularly imperative to establish an effective governance structure and mechanism in order to accomplish, maintain, and enhance the trust and confidence of all stakeholders engaging in the banking sector. In addition, banks have received strident criticism for their contribution to the global financial crisis in 2007–2009 (Nguyen et al. 2015). For example, ineffective monitoring and advising of directors can endanger the safety and soundness of the whole economic system. This motivates a need to monitor the health of the banking industry (Saeed and Izzeldin 2016) while assessing the influence of board attributes on corporate outcomes for banks. These discussions highlight the importance of designing effective board governance in banks so as to align the interests of management team with those of shareholders and other stakeholders (Shibani and De Fuentes 2017).

Last but not least, the banking sector is subject to intense scrutiny from several actors, especially in the stock market including investors, financial press and other stakeholders. The international banking system undergo rigorous regulatory control and supervision. While interventions (e.g., deposit insurance and protection by central banks and monetary authorities) could result in severe moral hazard problems (Macey and O'hara 2003), it is possible that banks, which are subject to intense regulatory scrutiny, may encounter additional pressures to design optimal contracts to reduce the conflict of interests between the banks and managers.

2.1.1 Why Islamic vs Conventional Banks?

Recent interests in governance and financial field are driven by Islamic banking and Islamic finance. This is as a result of the evolution of the Islamic mode of banking and its rapid growth in Muslim countries (Mollah et al. 2017). While conventional "western" banking system reveals many potential weaknesses over the subprime crisis, Islamic banking system displays their strength by remaining stable during the global crisis and seems not encounter solvency issues or large losses (Hasan and Dridi 2011; Beck et al. 2013; Mollah and Zaman 2015).

Furthermore, the annual growth rate of Islamic banks was recorded more than 20 per cent in 2012 (Faye et al. 2013), and grew approximately 50 per cent faster than the overall banking sector with an average growth rate of 17.6 per cent over the period of 2008–2012 (Ernst and Young 2012). Until the end of 2015, their assets worldwide in total reach $1.38 trillion (Islamic Financial Services Board 2017). This is projected to further increase to $6.5 trillion by 2020 (Islamic Financial Services Board 2010). Khan (2010) also reported 111 per cent of IBs' assets grew in the period of 1998 and 2005 whilst Conventional banks only grew by 6 per cent that implies a rapid growth of the Islamic banks over past decades as well as its potential enormous development in the future. As such, the impacts of the operations and policies of this type of religious-oriented bank on the global economy might be substantial.

In recent years, Islamic banks are no longer business entities operated only to fulfil the obligations of the Muslim community related to religion but also to cater the demands/needs of new clients (Ibrahim 2015). In addition, the governance reforms and the potential contributions of this banking model in restoring bank's creditability and stability in the global financial market. Accordingly, enhancing knowledge and understanding about issues around Islamic banking system is able to assist bank regulators in producing reflective guidelines in order to improve the managerial quality of such banks as well as enhance stability of international banking sector.

Along with the rapid growth of Islamic banks combined with fierce competition with Conventional banks in the same markets, this has spurred scholarly interest in examining the issues of market value, risk and stability, sustainability and financial strategies of Islamic banks in comparison to conventional ones (e.g., Čihák and Hesse 2010; Abedifar et al. 2013; Beck et al. 2013; Kabir et al. 2015; Mollah et al. 2017; Safiullah and Shamsuddin 2019). The recent banking crisis has also added to the attraction of Islamic banking to practitioners, monetary authorities, and academic scholars (Ibrahim 2015).

Furthermore, operations and functions of the conventional (western) banking system are principally based on profit maximisation, which is divergent from their Islamic counterparts being more ethically and socially responsible due to their religious identity (e.g., Mallin et al. 2014; Mollah and Zaman 2015; Mollah et al. 2017). This fact infers that the corporate governance structure and mechanism of banks ought to be different amongst such banking models. Indeed, the distinctive governance feature of the Islamic banks is the Shari'ah governance framework with the presence of a Shari'ah Committee (see details in the Chap. 4). This unique governance mechanism proposes a particular structure directed and controlled by this religious board (see Safieddine 2009; Quttainah et al. 2013). Islamic specialists, therefore, believed that the Shari'ah (or Islamic) principles underlying the contracts in Islamic banking lead to unique agency relationships (Safieddine 2009; Mallin et al. 2014).

The acknowledged differences of Islamic banks (i.e., Islamic corporate governance) to Conventional banks (i.e., western corporate governance) calls for further attention of academics and practitioners on comparing such two corporate governance systems and their potential different influences (i.e., board characteristics and attribute) on banking financial indicators and policies. In the view of their importance, it is stimulating that significantly growing studies have examined the differences of corporate governance of Islamic banks and their conventional counterparts (see details in the Chap. 4).

2.2 Governance in Banking

Generally, we refer corporate governance as the mechanisms which are used to solve agency conflicts and manage risks within the firm. Like non-financial firms, the concept of governance in banks also falls into two main categories: motivate mechanism and constraint mechanism (see Chen and Lin 2016):

- *Motivate mechanism:* is based on a bank's executives and their compensation (e.g., salary, stock options, rewards, etc.).
- *Constraint mechanism:* is related to the roles of a bank's shareholders or its board of directors. It is about the degree to which executives and managers are controlled by bank owners who have a tendency to monitor and control the bank agents to protect their self-interests (Morck et al. 2005) as they are less likely to diversify their own holdings (Shleifer and Vishny 1986).

In term of empirical evidence, several researchers (e.g., Amihud and Lev 1981; John et al. 2008; Laeven and Levine 2009) find that corporate governance factors such as compensation of executives, managers and directors, ownership structure and board-level attributes exert important influences on bank risk-taking, performance, market value as well as other outcomes. However, they find mixed and varying findings. For example, while Houston and James (1995) find an insignificant relationship between CEO compensation policies and bank risk-taking behaviour, John et al. (2000), Palia and Porter (2004), and Chen et al. (2006) find a negative link between such two variables. In addition, Balachandran et al. (2010), and Guo et al. (2015) provide some evidence on the positive effects of executive compensation on bank risk.

Governance in banks differs from that in non-financial (industrial) firms in the form of its effectiveness. Some examples for this are as follows:

- Due to some special features, governance issues within banking institutions are more intensified and the effectiveness of standard governance mechanisms might be alleviated (Laeven 2013; Levine 2004).
- Although the boards of directors are similar in terms of legal responsibilities between banks and firms, those in the former (i.e., banks) have to face more pressure as they must satisfy a wider range of internal and external stakeholders including shareholders, employees, customers, suppliers, creditors, government, among others (Adams 2012). Consequently, the challenges of boards of directors in banks are higher when the interests among different stakeholders are dissimilar or even conflicting. One of the good examples of this is the different interests between shareholders and bank regulators. While the former has some interests in profit maximisation, the latter is more concerned about the safety and soundness of the financial system. If banks aim to maximise firm profits, their risk-taking behaviour might be higher, and hence, the financial stability of banking institutions should be lower. The role of the boards of directors is, therefore, to balance interests and benefits among stakeholders, which is a difficult task assuming a low agency problem.

Furthermore, banking is a highly leveraged and regulated industry because of its important responsibilities in (i) protecting the rights of the depositors (investors), (ii) maintaining and improving the stability of the payment system within the economy, and (iii) decreasing the systematic risk of the whole financial system (Turlea et al. 2010). In addition to this, banking products, services, operations and other activities are more complex than those of non-financial firms. This, therefore, might create information asymmetry and prevent stakeholders from monitoring their operations and more importantly, behaviours and decisions of bank managers (Gebba and Aboelmaged 2016).

The higher information asymmetry within banks makes it more difficult for shareholders to control managers, and creditors to control the risk-shifting from shareholders to their shoulders. Also, the opacity of banks could reduce the effectiveness of building and designing incentive contracts. As such, managers of high opaque banks could easily design compensation packages that aim to offer them more benefits but not for the long-run success of their institution (Kose et al. 2016). As a result, it is essential to implement more specific and complicated governance mechanisms for banks, which might help safeguard the interests of different stakeholders in line with those of the public on a sustainable basis. For retail banks, the interest of depositors should be primary to that of shareholders.

Bank governance practice since 2010, according to Bank for International Settlements (Basel Committee on Banking Supervision 2015), has been improved and strengthened. Typically, banking firms have shown their better awareness and understanding of the crucial governance aspects involving effective board monitoring and supervision, thorough risk management mechanism, effective internal controls, compliance and others. They also demonstrate their improvement in reviewing collective skills and qualifications of board members (i.e., directors) and managers.

Furthermore, in modern board management and governance in banking, the presence of independent (or outside) directors on the boardroom has helped to promote the control and monitoring functions of the board and hence, limit managerial opportunism (Fama and Jensen 1983). As such, these independent directors play a vital role in the improvement of the quality and sincerity of managerial decisions, especially when independent directors in recent years are sitting in several boards across firms and even countries at the same time and this is argued to enhance their networking, experience, skills, information, and so on. That is to say, the consultancy and supervising functions of independent directors in modern boards have been significantly improved over time.

It can be also said that recruiting independent directors has become a common practice in the modern banking sector which requires a higher degree of monitoring and advising from the board than in the non-financial sector. The greater level of board independence has contributed to the development of modern bank performance, risk-taking and strategic decision-making. The practice and theory both show that more independence of the council could mitigate the likelihood of agreement with leaders that may enhance the protection of the interests of shareholders. This independence of boards can also ensure an effective follow-up and a greater degree of bank transparency (Frankel et al. 2011).

In a modern banking environment, role duality is also a common concern. If we follow the agency principles, we might support a separation between the Chairman and the CEO positions within a bank because this could enhance the supervising role of the board of directors. Duality can also reflect the lack of separation between control and managerial decisions (Fama and Jensen 1983). Subsequently, a combination of those two key senior roles is likely to create a rigorous individual power that will then hinder the proper ability of the council to conduct its responsibilities to manage the bank. In addition, the absence of Chair-CEO duality can prevent firms from making their decisions following the interests and benefits of a minority group of individuals (Ghazali 2010). Hence, agency problems can arise due to the role duality causing the accumulation of power in the hands of a single individual (i.e., Chair/CEO) and the lack of management (Gul and Lai 2002). Empirical evidence find mixed results on the duality aspect. Some report positive (Beasley et al. 2000) while others find a negative association between the Chairman-CEO duality and firm outcomes (Ntim et al. 2013).

There are other corporate governance characteristics and board attributes that a modern banking institution has been normally concerned about. They include:

- Board-related characteristics particularly diversity (e.g., gender, cultural, nationality), expertise, and compensation.
- CEO characteristics (e.g., gender, qualifications and education, age, marital status, experiences, skills, tenure, and compensation).
- Shareholding and ownership structure
- Committee characteristics (e.g., Audit, remuneration, risk management)
- And others

The Basel Committee on Banking Supervision (Emmenegger 2006) has emphasised the importance of establishing and continuously developing effective corporate governance practices to achieve and maintain public trust and confidence in the global banking sector.

From a traditional perspective, such governance is designed to align the interests of managers, shareholders and other stakeholders such as government, depositors, debtholders and customers. Bank governance can also offer some guarantees that managerial risk-taking should be falling within the bounds set by the risk tolerance of the principals (i.e., owners).

However, we also need to be concerned about the interactions of corporate governance and regulations as banking is a highly regulated industry (Gaganis et al. 2020). Two policies are imposed by regulators: Micro-prudential and macro-prudential. The purpose of both of them is to restrict bank-specific and systematic risk. Following this, effective risk management and corporate governance (i.e., mechanisms, structure and procedures) of banks should be designed by shareholders and supervisors (Tarullo 2014). Under the assumption that the interests (e.g., risk tolerance) among three main stakeholders, i.e., shareholders, managers and supervisors are aligned, bank high risks could be controlled by the interactions between internal and external mechanisms. Internal mechanism refers to the corporate governance mechanisms, structure and procedures while external mechanism refers to the regulations. As such, macroprudential regulations will play an important role in improving the effects of governance mechanisms on banking financial stability.

In summary, governance in the banking system has been subject to intense regulatory attention and community monitoring. There has been a growing body of empirical research focusing on various aspects of bank governance mechanisms, such as board structure and independence, CEO duality, board quality, financial expertise, busyness, compensation. All these factors are expected to exert significant impacts on bank outcomes.

References

Abedifar, P., P. Molyneux, and A. Tarazi. 2013. Risk in Islamic banking. *Review of Finance* 17 (6): 2035–2096.

Adams, R.B. 2012. Governance and the financial crisis. *International Review of Finance* 12 (1): 7–38.

Adams, R.B., and H. Mehran. 2012. Bank board structure and performance: Evidence for large bank holding companies. *Journal of Financial Intermediation* 21 (2): 243–267.

Aebi, V., G. Sabato, and M. Schmid. 2012. Risk management, corporate governance, and bank performance in the financial crisis. *Journal of Banking & Finance* 36 (12): 3213–3226.

Amihud, Y., and B. Lev. 1981. Risk reduction as a managerial motive for conglomerate mergers. *The Bell Journal of Economics* 12: 605–617.

Andres, D.P., and E. Vallelado. 2008. Corporate governance in banking: The role of the board of directors. *Journal of Banking & Finance* 32 (12): 2570–2580.

Balachandran, S., B. Kogut, H. Harnal, T. Gabriel, P. Glasserman, I. Gow, S. Meier, S. Penman, T. Rusticus, H. Spamann, and C. Thomas. 2010. Did executive compensation encourage excessive risk-taking in financial institutions. Retrieved February, 18, p.2012.

Basel Committee on Banking Supervision. 2015. Corporate governance principles for banks.

Beasley, M.S., J.V. Carcello, D.R. Hermanson, and P.D. Lapides. 2000. Fraudulent financial reporting: Consideration of industry traits and corporate governance mechanisms. *Accounting Horizons* 14 (4): 441–454.

Beck, T., A. Demirguc-Kunt, and O. Merrouche. 2013. Islamic vs. conventional banking: Business model, efficiency, and stability. *Journal of Banking & Finance* 37: 433–447.

Chen, H.J., and K.T. Lin. 2016. How do banks make the trade-offs among risks? The role of corporate governance. *Journal of Banking & Finance* 72: S39–S69.

Chen, C.R., T.L. Steiner, and A.M. Whyte. 2006. Does stock option-based executive compensation induce risk-taking? An analysis of the banking industry. *Journal of Banking & Finance* 30 (3): 915–945.

Čihák, M., and H. Hesse. 2010. Islamic banks and financial stability: An empirical analysis. *Journal of Financial Services Research* 38 (2): 95–113.

De Haan, J., and R. Vlahu. 2016. Corporate governance of banks: A survey. *Journal of Economic Surveys* 30 (2): 228–277.

Elyasiani, E., and L. Zhang. 2015. Bank holding company performance, risk, and "busy" board of directors. *Journal of Banking & Finance* 60: 239–251.

Emmenegger, S. 2006. The basel committee of banking supervision – A secret club of giants. In *The Regulation of International Financial Markets – Perspectives for Reform*, ed. Rainer Grote and Thilo Marauhn, 224–236. Cambridge: Cambridge University Press.

Erkens, D.H., M. Hung, and P. Matos. 2012. Corporate governance in the 2007–2008 financial crisis: Evidence from financial institutions worldwide. *Journal of Corporate Finance* 18 (2): 389–411.

Ernst and Young. 2012. World Islamic banking competitiveness report 2013. Available at: http://www.mifc.com/index.php?rp=ey_world_islamic_banking_competi
Fama, E.F., and M.C. Jensen. 1983. Agency problems and residual claims. *The Journal of Law and Economics* 26 (2): 327–349.
Faye, I., T. Triki, and T. Kangoye. 2013. The Islamic finance promises: Evidence from Africa. *Review of Development Finance* 3 (3): 136–151.
Frankel, R., S. McVay, and M. Soliman. 2011. Non-GAAP earnings and board independence. *Review of Accounting Studies* 16 (4): 719–744.
Gaganis, C., A. Lozano-Vivas, P. Papadimitri, and F. Pasiouras. 2020. Macroprudential policies, corporate governance and bank risk: Cross-country evidence. *Journal of Economic Behavior & Organization* 169: 126–142.
Gebba, T.R., and M.G. Aboelmaged. 2016. Corporate governance of UAE financial institutions: A comparative study between conventional and Islamic banks. *Journal of Applied Finance and Banking* 6 (5): 119.
Ghazali, N.A.M. 2010. Ownership structure, corporate governance and corporate performance in Malaysia. *International Journal of Commerce and Management*.
Gul, F.A., and K.W. Lai. 2002. Insider entrenchment, board leadership structure and informativeness of earnings. *Board Leadership Structure and Informativeness of Earnings*.
Guo, L., A. Jalal, and S. Khaksari. 2015. Bank executive compensation structure, risk taking and the financial crisis. *Review of Quantitative Finance and Accounting* 45 (3): 609–639.
Hasan, M., and J. Dridi. 2011. The effects of the global crisis on Islamic and conventional banks: A comparative study. *Journal of International Commerce, Economics and Policy* 2 (02): 163–200.
Houston, J.F., and C. James. 1995. CEO compensation and bank risk is compensation in banking structured to promote risk taking? *Journal of Monetary Economics* 36 (2): 405–431.
Ibrahim, M.H. 2015. Issues in Islamic banking and finance: Islamic banks, Shari'ah-compliant investment and sukuk. *Pacific-Basin Finance Journal* 34: 185–191.
Islamic Financial Services Board. 2010. *Islamic Finance and Global Financial Stability*.
———. 2017. Islamic financial services industry stability report. *Kuala Lumpur*.
John, K., T.A. John, and L.W. Senbet. 1991. Risk-shifting incentives of depository institutions: A new perspective on federal deposit insurance reform. *Journal of Banking & Finance* 15 (4–5): 895–915.
John, K., A. Saunders, and L.W. Senbet. 2000. A theory of bank regulation and management compensation. *The Review of Financial Studies* 13 (1): 95–125.
John, K., L. Litov, and B. Yeung. 2008. Corporate governance and risk-taking. *The Journal of Finance* 63 (4): 1679–1728.
Kabir, M.N., A. Worthington, and R. Gupta. 2015. Comparative credit risk in Islamic and conventional bank. *Pacific-Basin Finance Journal* 34: 327–353.
Khan, F. 2010. How 'Islamic' is Islamic banking? *Journal of Economic Behavior & Organization* 76 (3): 805–820.
Kirkpatrick, G. 2009. The corporate governance lessons from the financial crisis. *OECD Journal: Financial Market Trends* 2009 (1): 61–87.
Körner, T. 2017. Board accountability and risk taking in banking: Evidence from a quasi-experiment. *Journal of Financial Services Research* 52 (3): 155–190.
Kose, J., S. De Masi, and A. Paci. 2016. Corporate governance in banks. *Corporate Governance: An International Review* 24 (3): 303–321.
Laeven, L. 2013. Corporate governance: What's special about banks? *Annual Review of Financial Economics* 5 (1): 63–92.
Laeven, L., and R. Levine. 2009. Bank governance, regulation and risk taking. *Journal of Financial Economics* 93 (2): 259–275.
Levine, R. 2004. *The corporate governance of banks: A concise discussion of concepts and evidence*. The World Bank.
Macey, J., and M. O'hara. 2003. The corporate governance of banks. *Economic Policy Review* 9 (1).

Mallin, C., H. Farag, and K. Ow-Yong. 2014. Corporate social responsibility and financial performance in Islamic banks. *Journal of Economic Behavior & Organization* 103: S21–S38.

Mollah, S., and M. Zaman. 2015. Shari'ah supervision, corporate governance and performance: Conventional vs. Islamic banks. *Journal of Banking & Finance* 58: 418–435.

Mollah, S., M.K. Hassan, O. Al Farooque, and A. Mobarek. 2017. The governance, risk-taking, and performance of Islamic banks. *Journal of Financial Services Research* 51 (2): 195–219.

Morck, R., D. Wolfenzon, and B. Yeung. 2005. Corporate governance, economic entrenchment, and growth. *Journal of Economic Literature* 43 (3): 655–720.

Nguyen, D.D., J. Hagendorff, and A. Eshraghi. 2015. Which executive characteristics create value in banking? Evidence from appointment announcements. *Corporate Governance: An International Review* 23 (2): 112–128.

Ntim, C.G., S. Lindop, and D.A. Thomas. 2013. Corporate governance and risk reporting in South Africa: A study of corporate risk disclosures in the pre-and post-2007/2008 global financial crisis periods. *International Review of Financial Analysis* 30: 363–383.

O'Donnell, S., and D. Rodda. 2015. New realities of executive compensation in the Banking Industry: the importance of balancing differing perspectives. *White Paper MER-006, Meridian Compensation Partners.*

Palia, D., and R. Porter. 2004. The impact of capital requirements and managerial compensation on bank charter value. *Review of Quantitative Finance and Accounting* 23 (3): 191–206.

Pathan, S., and R. Faff. 2013. Does board structure in banks really affect their performance? *Journal of Banking & Finance* 37 (5): 1573–1589.

Quttainah, M.A., L. Song, and Q. Wu. 2013. Do Islamic banks employ less earnings management? *Journal of International Financial Management & Accounting* 24 (3): 203–233.

Saeed, M., and M. Izzeldin. 2016. Examining the relationship between default risk and efficiency in Islamic and conventional banks. *Journal of Economic Behavior & Organization* 132: 127–154.

Safieddine, A. 2009. Islamic financial institutions and corporate governance: New insights for agency theory. *Corporate Governance: An International Review* 17 (2): 142–158.

Safiullah, M., and A. Shamsuddin. 2019. Risk-adjusted efficiency and corporate governance: Evidence from Islamic and conventional banks. *Journal of Corporate Finance* 55: 105–140.

Sharfman, B.S. 2009. Enhancing the efficiency of board decision making: Lessons learned from the financial crisis of 2008. *Delaware Journal of Corporate Law (DJCL)* 34: 813.

Shibani, O., and C. De Fuentes. 2017. Differences and similarities between corporate governance principles in Islamic banks and Conventional banks. *Research in International Business and Finance* 42: 1005–1010.

Shleifer, A., and R.W. Vishny. 1986. Large shareholders and corporate control. *Journal of Political Economy*, *94*(3, Part 1), 461–488.

Sierra, G.E., E. Talmor, and J.S. Wallace. 2006. An examination of multiple governance forces within bank holding companies. *Journal of Financial Services Research* 29 (2): 105–123.

Tarullo, D. 2014. Corporate governance and bank regulation. *The Corporate Board*, pp. 1–5.

Turlea, E., M. Mocanu, and R. Carmen. 2010. Corporate governance in the banking industry. *Accounting and Management Information Systems* 9 (3): 379.

Chapter 3
Setting the Stage: Board Busyness as a Matter of Modern Banking Context

As The Results of the recent revolution of the corporate governance system globally after the global financial crisis 2007–2009, the legal and moral accountabilities have been progressively shifted to the shoulders of bank directors and executives. Consequently, taking too many directorships as a current trend has become a special concern of modern financial corporations. It is likely to affect the directors' and executives' performance over bank financial stability and decision-making. Furthermore, the current economic and social situations are very complicated and uncertain, especially under the unpredicted COVID-19 pandemic waves. Hence, the banking sector has been facing some huge challenges which contribute to the substantial increase in the workloads of directors and executives leading to the high demand for experienced and skilled directors. Meanwhile, the associated reputational and litigation risks are mitigating the pool of available directors. To lure directors, firms are offering attractive compensation packages including both cash remuneration and equity incentive compensation. Such payments appear to attract those directors to accept, either voluntarily or involuntarily, more board seats given that the supply of directors in the labour market is reducing. However, higher pay and more board appointments can induce weak governance structures, giving rise to agency problems (Linck et al. 2009; Core et al. 1999).

As almost all projects of banks are related to some levels of risks, the lax involvement of those directors and executives in bank activities is wagering on the firm's financial distress and stability. To make rational and sound investment decisions, directors and executives are required to possess sufficient specialised knowledge, industry experience and substantial efforts to effectively monitor and advise management. Arguably, those requirements may practically be not obtained for "extremely" "busy" directors, indeed, even for less "busy" directors. "Busy" directors are likely to have relatively less time available to devote effort to collect information about the business's affairs or acquire related knowledge (Hart 1995).

In this ever-progressively, evolving and complex financial world, directors can be drowned by a tsunami of information, board meetings and tasks and swiped away by

V. Quang Trinh, *Fundamentals of Board Busyness and Corporate Governance*, Contributions to Management Science,
https://doi.org/10.1007/978-3-030-89228-9_3

the convergence of the numerous unpredicted financial turmoil and dramatic inauspicious variations in the universal political and economic circumstances. Consequently, there is a likelihood that the number of "busy" directors who shirk their responsibilities is increasing. This ostensible trend has also been incurred for Shari'ah scholars who are appointed on the religious boards of Islamic banks (Safiullah and Shamsuddin 2019). The standard of Accounting and Auditing Organizations for Islamic Financial Institutions (AAOIFI) defines that Shari'ah advisors as specialised jurists who are responsible for directing, reviewing and supervising all transactions, policies and activities of Islamic banks that are associated with Islamic finance. By doing so, these advisors could ensure that such transactions, policies and activities comply with Islamic rules and principles (Lahsasna 2010). Similarly, paying high compensation to directors may lead them to not challenge management policies that potentially enhances firm value (Sharma 2011).

Multiple directorships in both non-financial and financial firms have been one of the most popular subjects of academic debate. Based on the above two mature theories which are the agency and resource dependence perspectives (see Chap. 1), scholars suggest two competing hypotheses on the outcome of organisations with "busy" directors and executives: Reputation Hypothesis and Busyness Hypothesis. They assert that multiple directorships are not only observed as a positive indicator for the benefits of directors but also as a negative sign for the risks of directors being stretched thin.

3.1 Reputation Theory

Under the resource dependence perspective, reputation hypothesis on directors' (as well as executives') multiple directorships are established. This hypothesis postulates the following benefits of multiple directorships:

1. The number of outside board seats (directorships) held by directors is a proxy for their reputation capital in the external labour market (Fama and Jensen 1983b; Zajac and Westphal 1996; Vafeas 1999; Brickley et al. 1999; Harris and Shimizu 2004). It is related to their managerial performance as monitoring specialists (Fich and Shivdasani 2006).
2. Multiple board appointments can signal director quality (Fama and Jensen 1983b) and may improve board decision making ability and lead to a positive outcome by firms for which directors hold more outside board seats (Ahn et al. 2010).
3. "Busy" directors who serves in many firms at the same time can be a source of valuable knowledge, experience, and business connections, and hence, they can provide better advice (Kaplan and Reishus 1990; Gilson 1990; Haunschild 1993; Zajac and Westphal 1996; Haunschild and Beckman 1998; Vafeas 1999; Ferris et al. 2003; Harris and Shimizu 2004).
4. The social ties of "busy" directors make them excellent advisors and value-enhancing directors (Field et al. 2013).

Those resources above can reduce bank uncertainty (Pfeffer 1972), transaction costs (Williamson 1984) and mitigate dependency of firms on external contingencies (Pfeffer and Salancik 1978). If this is the case, they should help in increasing the level of board monitoring, lessening agency costs, and protecting shareholder interests. As a result, corporations with such "busy" directors might exhibit superior performance and board decision making (Fama and Jensen 1983b). This, in turn, is beneficial to the bank financial stability, market valuations, corporate policies and decision-making quality.

Prior research has documented the positive relationships between "busy" directors and corporate outcomes, which supports the reputation hypothesis. Pioneering evidence consistent with this assertion can be found in the studies of Fama (1980), Fama and Jensen (1983a), Mace (1986), Kaplan and Reishus (1990), Gilson (1990), Lang and Lockhart (1990), Shivdasani (1993), Beasley (1996), Mizruchi (1996), Burt (1997), Cotter et al. (1997), Haunschild and Beckman (1998), Brickley et al. (1999), Brown and Maloney (1999) and Miwa and Ramseyer (2000), among others.

- Fama (1980) and Fama and Jensen (1983a) were among the first scholars to introduce the concepts and knowledge of multiple directorships. They generally certify the outstanding ability of individual directors in the external labour market because their appointments to numerous boards help them to gain diversified experience and exceptional advisory ability, and to extend their business networks and contacts. Corporations with such directors, hence, might exhibit superior performance and board decision making.
- Mace (1986) further finds that multiple directorships held by an executive could add more value to the company since they can permit this executive to either establish a wide network or scrutinise corporate relations.
- Kaplan and Reishus (1990) report that top managers who reduce firm dividends tend to obtain 50 per cent less external directorships.
- Gilson (1990), Shivdasani (1993) and Harford (2003) conclude that directors related to better-performing firms hold more board seats while those related to poorly performing firms hold fewer board seats.
- Beasley (1996) finds a negative relationship between firms with "busy" outside directors and their likelihood of financial statement fraud. This implies that these firms are less likely to commit fraud.
- Booth and Deli (1996) find that CEOs holding multiple directorships can transfer decision rights to their eventual successor.
- Cotter et al. (1997) report that the merger premium offered will be greater if a merger target's board comprises "busy" individuals. In the same line with these research, Haunschild and Beckman (1998) argue that such directors positively contribute to the entire corporate system by the dissemination of innovations throughout corporate networks.
- Brickley et al. (1999) find a positive relationship between a retired CEO who sits on his own board or on other boards, and his firm's performance while he was the CEO.

- Brown and Maloney (1999) also report a superior acquisitions' returns of companies recruiting multiple directors.
- Miwa and Ramseyer (2000) document that during the first decade of the twentieth century, "busy" directors are strongly associated with firm success in the cotton spinning industry in Japan.
- Lang and Lockhart (1990), Palmer et al. (1993) and Ahuja (2000) claim that indirect interlocks are considered as a form of board social capital which has a significantly positive effect on firm outcomes (e.g., patents development). This is subsequently supported by numerous studies such as Mizruchi (1996), Burt (1997), Carpenter and Westphal (2001), Hillman and Dalziel (2003). These works generally find that board interlocks of directors can add value to the firm because they could enhance the board advising and supervising effectiveness on managers. Also, interlocks are found to influence board ability through improving directors' knowledge, skills and expertise, which is elucidated by agency and resource dependence theories.
- While Ferris et al. (2003) find no evidence that such directors neglect their board responsibilities or harm firm performance, there is an evidence that "busy" directors are important sources of extensive knowledge and represent an important complement to inside directors (Harris and Shimizu 2004), and contribute positively to firm value (Field et al. 2013).
- In a similar vein, Elyasiani and Zhang (2015) indicate that bank holding companies with more "busy" directors have desirable effects on their financial performance and have lower total, market, and idiosyncratic risk.
- Although Lei and Deng (2014) document a positive relation between independent directors' multiple directorships and firm value, they find that the busyness effect is stronger under better governance standards and that the positive effect declines at higher levels of busyness.
- Field et al. (2013) emphasise that directors with multiple board seats are excellent advisors are on demand by newly public venture-backed firms.
- Chakravarty and Rutherford (2017) find that, through a hostile takeover framework, "busy" outside directors tend to mitigate a corporate hostile takeover vulnerability and US firm's cost of debt.
- Chou and Feng (2018) further explore a positive relation between "busy" boards and dividend pay-outs when non-financial US firms have more limited investment opportunities. They also conclude that board busyness leads to a more efficient use of cash, and providing direct benefits to shareholders. The studies mentioned above advocate for a positive alignment between board members' multiple directorships and shareholders' interests in the non-financial sector.
- Among others.

3.2 Busyness Theory

However, the contribution of a director to the board advisory and monitoring performance not only depends on their knowledge or skills, but also on the time availability to perform their duties and the time for preparing of the board meetings, for example. Although reputation theory is consistent with the resource dependence predictions (Hillman and Dalziel 2003), it is only part of the story (Laurent 2016), and so it is an on-going debate. Prior reviews of multiple directorships of directors (and executives) show an overwhelmingly strong opposite view (the Busyness Hypothesis) which is derived from agency theory. The arguments are as below:

1. "Busy" directors may not have the necessary reputation and networking contacts that are needed to generate benefits to the institution (Jackling and Johl 2009).
2. "Busy" directors have been criticised as being ineffective, and that a reduction in their workload is associated with improved operating profits and higher market to book ratios (Hauser 2018).
3. To competently contribute and effectively discharge monitoring responsibilities, they are required to spend a lot more time than just time spent in board meetings (Trinh et al. 2021). However, outsiders may not do a very good job of monitoring as they are "over-boarded" directors, sitting on many boards, and likely have relatively less time available to devote effort to collect information about the business's affairs or acquire related knowledge—above that provided by management (Hart 1995). As such, they are associated with weak governance structures, giving rise to agency problems (Core et al. 1999).

The theory therefore predicts an inverse relationship between the board's busyness and the corporate outcome (Fich and Shivdasani 2006; Ahn et al. 2010; Cooper and Uzun 2012; Cashman et al. 2012). It claims that accumulation of board seats overcommits a director (Fich and Shivdasani 2006; Jiraporn et al. 2008; Jackling and Johl 2009; Cashman et al. 2012; Falato et al. 2014; Zhang 2016). Directors who serve on multiple boards become so "busy" (e.g., compromise their responsibilities and neglect their duties) that they are unable to monitor management effectively. This causes decline in firm value (Falato et al. 2014; Core et al. 1999; Shivdasani and Yermack 1999; Eisenhardt 1989) and is detrimental to a bank's financial stability, market valuations, corporate policies and decision-making quality.

Therefore, a line of thought within the existing literature has provided some evidence for the busyness hypothesis.

- Earlier studies, such as Eisenhardt (1989), Core et al. (1999) and Shivdasani and Yermack (1999) argue the potential risks and consequences associated with multiple board appointments. They generally indicate that directors sitting on several boards affect negatively firm performance. They emphasise that these directors tend to overstretched themselves and spend less time on each individual board. They may also compromise their responsibilities and neglect their duties, resulting in ineffective advising and monitoring management. This causes decline in firm value.

- Forbes and Milliken (1999) contend that less time to prepare readings distributed in advance of meetings also reduces the level of his expected involvement.
- Granovetter (1973) argues that multiple indirect interlocks are observed as weak ties which are only influential if the boardroom depends upon them as final connection tools.
- Recent work on this negative effect of busyness (e.g., Fich and Shivdasani 2006; Jiraporn et al. 2008; Jackling and Johl 2009; Cashman et al. 2012; Falato et al. 2014; Zhang 2016) criticise that a "busy" director is too busy to monitor and is unlikely to provide thoughtful advice to and exercise active control over executives; and hence, he/she is detrimental to monitoring quality, business valuation and shareholder wealth.
- Chen (2008) finds that "busy" directors have a positive (negative) impact on the performance of firms having low (high) agency conflicts and high (low) growth opportunities.
- Falato et al. (2014) find that busyness functioning of outside directors is detrimental to board monitoring quality. However, Cashman et al. (2012) conclude that the conflicting findings of previous research are potentially the result of differences in both the samples studied and the empirical designs.
- Jackling and Johl (2009) and Fich and Shivdasani (2006) contend that over-boarded directors are related to weak corporate governance and thus to poor firm performance. News about an overcommitted director leaving the board positively affected the returns announcement of the incumbent firms. In contrast, news about a director accepting a third board seat adversely impacted the announcement returns. Likewise, Jiraporn et al. (2008) find that overcommitted directors suffer larger diversification discounts and lower firm value. Ahn et al. (2010) then report that firms experienced more negative acquisition announcement returns if they employed over-boarded directors.
- Faleye et al. (2011) find a positive relationship between "busy" directors and CEO remunerations. Along the same lines, Hauser (2018) finds that a reduction in the number of board seats held by outside directors will increase the earnings, book-to-market ratio and pay-performance sensitivity in the CEO compensation contracts.
- Sharma (2011) finds that "busy" outside directors are negatively associated with a firm's dividend policy. Specifically, "busy" outside directors tend to reduce the propensity to pay a dividend.

Below provides additional arguments and important evidence that are consistent with the busyness hypothesis (Ahn et al. 2010). For example:

- The distracted "busy" directors have higher meeting absence and a higher likelihood of yielding less prestigious directorship (Zhang 2016). They are too busy to monitor, unlikely to provide thoughtful advice to and active control over executives, and are detrimental to monitoring quality, business valuation, and shareholder wealth (Fich and Shivdasani 2006; Jiraporn et al. 2008; Jackling and Johl 2009; Cashman et al. 2012; Falato et al. 2014; Zhang 2016).

- "Busy" directors have a positive (negative) impact on the performance of firms having low (high) agency conflicts and high (low) growth opportunities (Chen 2008).
- Over-boarded ("busy") directors are related to weak corporate governance, thus poor firm performance (Jackling and Johl 2009; Fich and Shivdasani 2006). The news that overcommitted director leaves the board affected positively on announcement returns of the incumbent firms. In contrast, the news that a director accepts a third board seat impacted adversely on announcement returns.
- Overcommitted directors suffer a larger diversification discounts and lower firm value (Jiraporn et al. 2008). Ahn et al. (2010) then report that firms experienced more negative acquisition announcement returns if they employed over-boarded directors. Faleye et al. (2011) find a positive relationship between "busy" directors and CEO remunerations. Along the same lines, Hauser (2018) believe that a reduction in the number of board seats held by outside directors will increase earnings, market to book ratio, and pay-performance sensitivity in CEO compensation contracts.

3.3 Setting the Stage: Board Busyness as a Matter of Banking Context

Reconciling the two opposing hypotheses, Jiraporn et al. (2009) indicate a nonlinear U-Shape association between overcommitted directors and the number of board committees they serve on. Specifically, at lower degrees of busyness, directors holding more board seats are likely to serve on fewer board committees, and this idea is supported by the busyness hypothesis. However, at higher degrees of busyness, directors holding more board seats tend to serve on a higher number of board committees, and this idea is supported by the reputation hypothesis. They also emphasise that "busy" directors tend to miss their board meetings.

The discussion above outlines the on-going debate on the benefits and detriments of multiple directorships in the corporate literature. However, financial institutions like banks seem to be more complex than those non-financial firms due to their larger size, more diversified and higher leverage (Elyasiani and Zhang 2015; Coles et al. 2008). They are therefore likely to require more advising and monitoring from their board of directors (Klein 1998). However, they face several problems involved in lack of decent and well corporate governance structure and mechanism, which may increase bank cost of capital and further reduce productivity growth (Toufik 2015).

Additionally, banks also have unique features such as stricter regulation of banking industry and potential for contagion within banks and from banks to the real economy. This implies dissimilar effects of bank board's effectiveness and its relation to performance and risk factors as well as market valuations and financial policies, compared to non-financial firms (Elyasiani and Zhang 2015; Macey and O'Hara 2003; Adams and Mehran 2003). Firm managers need to be aware of different forms of governance to control and coordinate the actions of various parties (i.e., stakeholders) to ensure the firm success and further create public confidence (Toufik 2015). Also, this suggests an importance of evaluation of board busyness's effects in banking industry due to its high monitoring and advising demands.

Prior literature started from Macey and O'Hara (2003) has underlined the dissimilarities between corporate governance of industrial (non-financial) institutions and their financial counterparts like banks. The former is governed according to the Anglo-American model, in which the exclusive focus of corporate governance is to maximise shareholder (owner) wealth, while corporate governance of the latter (i.e., banks) fits into a variant of the Franco-German paradigm where the fiduciary duties of boards go beyond shareholders to include other stakeholders such as bondholders, depositors, regulators, buyers of bank guarantee services (e.g., loan commitments, standby letters of credit). If the interests of this group of stakeholders are ignored, they may take actions harmful to the bank's interest (John and John 1993; Bai and Elyasiani 2013). Such unique feature of corporate governance challenges banks as these banks must balance the shareholders' demands as a value-maximising business and the public's interests (Mehran et al. 2011; Mehran and Mollineaux 2012).

It is presumed to run to benefit stakeholders in addition to its intermediary function (O'Hara 1983). These challenges can promote higher agency conflicts among stakeholders and bank managers. For example, if a bank is publicly traded on stock markets, it has to satisfy investors and follow strict banking regulations due to its economic importance (i.e., potential for contagion within banks and from banks to the real economy). Whilst investors tend to demand a bank's profitability, regulators are more likely to demand a bank's soundness and financial stability. Thereby, management of a bank must satisfy demands of both parties that are in most cases in conflict with each other. Positive net present value NPV (profitable) projects may not necessarily increase the quality of financial intermediations because profitability is directly associated with risky investments. As such, a bank's boards should be responsible for controlling optimal levels of risk to accomplish target profits, which needs bank-specific and macroeconomic inside information and expertise. Therefore, the board has an essential duty to balance the objective of profitability and financial stability, via optimal risk-taking (Kutubi et al. 2018), leading to its greater degree of pressure in advising and monitoring managers (Klein 1998). Such complexity of bank governance implies dissimilar influences of the bank board's effectiveness on stability, market valuations and financial policies relative to industrial entities (Macey and O'Hara 2003; Adams and Mehran 2003; Coles et al. 2008; Elyasiani and Zhang 2015; Kutubi et al. 2018).

In practice, banks today face to several problems involved in lack of decent and well internal corporate governance mechanism which could increase their cost of capital and further reduce their productivity growth (Toufik 2015). Consequently, research of internal governance quality (e.g., board directorships, size, independence, CEO duality, ownership structure) within banking sector is imperative in improving its managerial quality and corporate governance structure.

Evidences on the effects of multiple board appointments of directors in banking sector are growing but still limited. Most of prior banking literature mainly focuses on examining the effect of other board characteristics (i.e., board size, board independence) and CEO characterises (i.e., CEO duality, CEO Tenure) on bank performance and risk-taking.

- Sierra et al. (2006) find that banks with strong boards of directos exhibit higher performance whilst Pathan (2009) argue that these banks exhibit excessive bank risk-taking behaviour.
- Adams and Mehran (2012) report a positive effect of board size on performance but they cannot find the positive impact of outside directors like conclusions of Cornett et al. (2009).
- Wintoki et al. (2012) also cannot identify any link between board size or board independence and bank performance. Meanwhile, Andres and Vallelado (2008) find a positive impact of both board size and independence on bank performance whilst Pathan and Faff (2013) report a negative effect.
- Pi and Timme (1993) find an adverse association between Chair-CEO duality and bank operating performance in the US market. They find no relationship between such performance indicators and the board independence as well as block shareholder ownership.
- Booth et al. (2002) furthermore find that an increase in insider ownership leads to a reduction in the proportion of outside directors, and a lower probability of CEO-Chairman duality.
- Andres and Vallelado (2008) employ an international sample (i.e., Canada, France, the UK, Italy, Spain and the US) of 69 large commercial banks to investigate the influences of bank performance and board meetings, board size and independence for a period of 10 years from 1995. They interestingly explore that while the relationship between board meetings and bank performance is significantly positive, the effects of board size/independence on such indicators are inverted U-shaped.
- Pathan (2009) finds a robust positive linkage between small, less restrictive boards of directors and risk indicators of 212 large US bank holding companies from 1997 to 2004.
- Cornett et al. (2009) find that board independence is likely to constrain earnings management of US bank holding companies from 1992 to 2002.
- Adams and Mehran (2012) use another US sample of 35 listed banks over the period of 1986–1999 and find a positive impact of board size and performance.

Cooper and Uzun (2012) were first to study the direct effect of multiple board appointments on bank risk measures (idiosyncratic risk and total risks) and they find a positive relationship between them. This means that multiple directorships of directors tend to increase bank risk-taking behaviour of banks, supported for busyness hypothesis. However, their study is only conducted in US stock markets (NYSE, AMEX, and NASDAQ) during crisis period of 2006.

Elyasiani and Zhang (2015) then continued extending the literature to banking firms in the US market by investigating association between "busy" directors and bank holding company's performance and risks. Their results are contrasting to the findings of Cooper and Uzun (2012). They find that the presence of "busy" directors has positive impacts on bank performance indicators (return on equity, Tobin's Q and EBIT over total assets) and negative influences on risk indicators (total, market, idiosyncratic, credit and default risks). This evidence supports for reputational hypothesis that "busy" directors own more extensive knowledge, information, and rich experience because of their wide interactions with many industries in the economy system, than their "non-busy" counterparts. As such, these directors should serve as a catalyst in their interactions as board members.

More importantly, Elyasiani and Zhang also argue that "busy" bank directors are often monitored more intensively by regulators and they are often unwilling to take high risk as it may affect their reputation as expert directors, and hence, they tend to become more effective board members. In addition, they also emphasise that during crisis 2007–2009, performance benefits are likely to strengthen whilst risk benefits tend to be weakened. Interestingly, "busy" directors may not become problem directors who fail to attend at least 75 per cent of meetings. They often attend more meetings in bank holding companies than non-financial firms.

Furthermore, Jackson and Fang (2014) find an evidence that social networks can provide bank CEOs an efficient information channel which helped them take lower risk over the recent global banking crisis 2008. Indeed, they indicate a significantly positive effect of board social networks in mitigating the personal wealth loss of bank CEOs during the turmoil.

By reconciling mixed results in the previous literature on the busyness-performance linkage, Kutubi et al. (2018) have examined the relationship between board busyness and bank performance and risk in concentrated ownership and weak-external governance regimes in South East Asia. They find an inverted U-shaped association between "busy" boards and bank performance and a U-shaped association between such board and bank financial risk. However, when controlling for types of directors (inside and outside), they find only significant effects of "busy" inside directors on bank performance and risk.

More recently, a series of research by Trinh et al. has been conducted to examine the effects of board busyness on different outcomes of dual banking system. Details are provided in Chap. 5 (Sects. 5.3.1 to 5.3.5).

References

Adams, R., and H. Mehran, 2003. Is corporate governance different for bank holding companies?. *SSRN*.

Adams, R.B., and H. Mehran. 2012. Bank board structure and performance: Evidence for large bank holding companies. *Journal of Financial Intermediation* 21 (2): 243–267.

Ahn, S., P. Jiraporn, and Y.S. Kim. 2010. Multiple directorships and acquirer returns. *Journal of Banking & Finance* 34 (9): 2011–2026.

Ahuja, G. 2000. Collaboration networks, structural holes, and innovation: A longitudinal study. *Administrative Science Quarterly* 45 (3): 425–455.

Andres, D.P., and E. Vallelado. 2008. Corporate governance in banking: The role of the board of directors. *Journal of Banking & Finance* 32 (12): 2570–2580.

Bai, G., and E. Elyasiani. 2013. Bank stability and managerial compensation. *Journal of Banking & Finance* 37 (3): 799–813.

Beasley, M.S. 1996. An empirical analysis of the relation between the board of director composition and financial statement fraud. *Accounting Review* 71: 443–465.

Booth, J.R., and D.N. Deli. 1996. Factors affecting the number of outside directorships held by CEOs. *Journal of Financial Economics* 40 (1): 81–104.

Booth, J.R., M.M. Cornett, and H. Tehranian. 2002. Boards of directors, ownership, and regulation. *Journal of Banking & Finance* 26 (10): 1973–1996.

Brickley, J.A., J.S. Linck, and J.L. Coles. 1999. What happens to CEOs after they retire? New evidence on career concerns, horizon problems, and CEO incentives. *Journal of Financial Economics* 52 (3): 341–377.

Brown, W.O., and M.T. Maloney. 1999. *Exit, voice, and the role of corporate directors: Evidence from acquisition performance*. Available at SSRN 160308.

Burt, R.S. 1997. A note on social capital and network content. *Social Networks* 19 (4): 355–373.

Carpenter, M.A., and J.D. Westphal. 2001. The strategic context of external network ties: Examining the impact of director appointments on board involvement in strategic decision making. *Academy of Management Journal* 44 (4): 639–660.

Cashman, G.D., S.L. Gillan, and C. Jun. 2012. Going overboard? On busy directors and firm value. *Journal of Banking & Finance* 36 (12): 3248–3259.

Chakravarty, S., and L.G. Rutherford. 2017. Do busy directors influence the cost of debt? An examination through the lens of takeover vulnerability. *Journal of Corporate Finance* 43: 429–443.

Chen, C.W. 2008. *Two Essays on Multiple Directorships*. University of South Florida: Graduate Theses and Dissertations. http://scholarcommons.usf.edu/etd/171. [Accessed 15 Mar. 2017].

Chou, T.K., and H.L. Feng. 2018. Multiple directorships and the value of cash holdings. *Review of Quantitative Finance and Accounting*, pp. 1–37.

Coles, J.L., N.D. Daniel, and L. Naveen. 2008. Boards: Does one size fit all? *Journal of Financial Economics* 87 (2): 329–356.

Cooper, E., and H. Uzun. 2012. Directors with a full plate: The impact of busy directors on bank risk. *Managerial Finance* 38 (6): 571–586.

Core, J.E., R.W. Holthausen, and D.F. Larcker. 1999. Corporate governance, chief executive officer compensation, and firm performance. *Journal of Financial Economics* 51 (3): 371–406.

Cornett, M.M., J.J. McNutt, and H. Tehranian. 2009. Corporate governance and earnings management at large US bank holding companies. *Journal of Corporate Finance* 15 (4): 412–430.

Cotter, J.F., A. Shivdasani, and M. Zenner. 1997. Do independent directors enhance target shareholder wealth during tender offers? *Journal of Financial Economics* 43 (2): 195–218.

Eisenhardt, K.M. 1989. Agency theory: An assessment and review. *Academy of Management Review* 14 (1): 57–74.

Elyasiani, E., and L. Zhang. 2015. Bank holding company performance, risk, and "busy" board of directors. *Journal of Banking & Finance* 60: 239–251.

Falato, A., D. Kadyrzhanova, and U. Lel. 2014. Distracted directors: Does board busyness hurt shareholder value? *Journal of Financial Economics* 113 (3): 404–426.

Faleye, O., R. Hoitash, and U. Hoitash. 2011. The costs of intense board monitoring. *Journal of Financial Economics* 101 (1): 160–181.

Fama, E.F. 1980. Agency problems and the theory of the firm. *Journal of Political Economy* 88 (2): 288–307.

Fama, E.F., and M.C. Jensen. 1983a. Separation of ownership and control. *The Journal of Law and Economics* 26 (2): 301–325.

———. 1983b. Agency problems and residual claims. *The Journal of Law and Economics* 26 (2): 327–349.

Ferris, S.P., M. Jagannathan, and A.C. Pritchard. 2003. Too busy to mind the business? Monitoring by directors with multiple board appointments. *The Journal of Finance* 58 (3): 1087–1111.

Fich, E.M., and A. Shivdasani. 2006. Are busy boards effective monitors? *The Journal of Finance* 61 (2): 689–724.
Field, L., M. Lowry, and A. Mkrtchyan. 2013. Are busy boards detrimental? *Journal of Financial Economics* 109 (1): 63–82.
Forbes, D.P., and F.J. Milliken. 1999. Cognition and corporate governance: Understanding boards of directors as strategic decision-making groups. *Academy of Management Review* 24 (3): 489–505.
Gilson, S.C. 1990. Bankruptcy, boards, banks, and blockholders: Evidence on changes in corporate ownership and control when firms default. *Journal of Financial Economics* 27 (2): 355–387.
Granovetter, M.S. 1973. The strength of weak ties. *American Journal of Sociology* 78 (6): 1360–1380.
Harford, J. 2003. Takeover bids and target directors' incentives: The impact of a bid on directors' wealth and board seats. *Journal of Financial Economics* 69 (1): 51–83.
Harris, I.C., and K. Shimizu. 2004. Too busy to serve? An examination of the influence of overboarded directors. *Journal of Management Studies* 41 (5): 775–798.
Hart, S.L. 1995. A natural-resource-based view of the firm. *Academy of Management Review* 20 (4): 986–1014.
Haunschild, P.R. 1993. Interorganizational imitation: The impact of interlocks on corporate acquisition activity. *Administrative Science Quarterly* 38: 564–592.
Haunschild, P.R., and C.M. Beckman. 1998. When do interlocks matter?: Alternate sources of information and interlock influence. *Administrative Science Quarterly* 43: 815–844.
Hauser, R. 2018. Busy directors and firm performance: Evidence from mergers. *Journal of Financial Economics* 128 (1): 16–37.
Hillman, A.J., and T. Dalziel. 2003. Boards of directors and firm performance: Integrating agency and resource dependence perspectives. *Academy of Management Review* 28 (3): 383–396.
Jackling, B., and S. Johl. 2009. Board structure and firm performance: Evidence from India's top companies. *Corporate Governance: An International Review* 17 (4): 492–509.
Jackson, D., and F. Fang. 2014. CEO networks and bank risk taking. *Banking and Finance Review.*
Jiraporn, P., Y.S. Kim, and W.N. Davidson III. 2008. Multiple directorships and corporate diversification. *Journal of Empirical Finance* 15 (3): 418–435.
Jiraporn, P., M. Singh, and C.I. Lee. 2009. Ineffective corporate governance: Director busyness and board committee memberships. *Journal of Banking & Finance* 33 (5): 819–828.
John, T.A., and K. John. 1993. Top-management compensation and capital structure. *The Journal of Finance* 48 (3): 949–974.
Kaplan, S.N., and D. Reishus. 1990. Outside directorships and corporate performance. *Journal of Financial Economics* 27 (2): 389–410.
Klein, A. 1998. Firm performance and board committee structure. *The Journal of Law and Economics* 41 (1): 275–304.
Kutubi, S.S., K. Ahmed, and H. Khan. 2018. Bank performance and risk-taking—Does directors' busyness matter? *Pacific-Basin Finance Journal* 50: 184–199.
Lahsasna, A. 2010. *Introduction to fatwa, Shariah supervision & governance in Islamic finance.* CERT Publications Sdn. Bhd.
Lang, J.R., and D.E. Lockhart. 1990. Increased environmental uncertainty and changes in board linkage patterns. *Academy of Management Journal* 33 (1): 106–128.
Laurent, L. 2016. *Are Credit Suisse's Directors Overstretched?* [online] Bloomberg Gadfly. Available at: https://www.bloomberg.com/gadfly/articles/2016-04-18/credit-suisse-surprise-loss-raises-flag-on-directors-commitments. [Accessed 30 Dec. 2016].
Lei, A.C., and J. Deng. 2014. Do multiple directorships increase firm value? Evidence from independent directors in Hong Kong. *Journal of International Financial Management & Accounting* 25 (2): 121–181.
Linck, J.S., J.M. Netter, and T. Yang. 2009. The effects and unintended consequences of the Sarbanes-Oxley Act on the supply and demand for directors. *The Review of Financial Studies* 22 (8): 3287–3328.

Mace, M. 1986. *Directors: Myth and reality*. Boston, MA: Harvard Business School Press.
Macey, J., and M. O'hara. 2003. The corporate governance of banks. Economic Policy Review, 9 (1).
Mehran, H., and L. Mollineaux. 2012. Corporate governance of financial institutions. *Annual Review of Financial Economics* 4 (1): 215–232.
Mehran, H., A. Morrison, and J. Shapiro. 2011. Corporate governance and banks: What have we learned from the financial crisis?. *FRB of New York Staff Report.*
Miwa, Y., and J.M. Ramseyer. 2000. Corporate governance in transitional economies: lessons from the prewar Japanese cotton textile industry. *The Journal of Legal Studies* 29 (1): 171–203.
Mizruchi, M.S. 1996. What do interlocks do? An analysis, critique, and assessment of research on interlocking directorates. *Annual Review of Sociology* 22 (1): 271–298.
O'hara, M. 1983. A dynamic theory of the banking firm. *The Journal of Finance* 38 (1): 127–140.
Palmer, D.A., P.D. Jennings, and X. Zhou. 1993. Late adoption of the multidivisional form by large US corporations: Institutional, political, and economic accounts. *Administrative Science Quarterly*, pp. 100–131.
Pathan, S. 2009. Strong boards, CEO power and bank risk-taking. *Journal of Banking & Finance* 33 (7): 1340–1350.
Pathan, S., and R. Faff. 2013. Does board structure in banks really affect their performance? *Journal of Banking & Finance* 37 (5): 1573–1589.
Pfeffer, J. 1972. Size and composition of corporate boards of directors: The organization and its environment. *Administrative Science Quarterly*, pp. 218–228.
Pfeffer, J., and G.R. Salancik. 1978. *The External Control of Organisations: A Resource Dependence Perspective*. New York: Harper & Row.
Pi, L., and S.G. Timme. 1993. Corporate control and bank efficiency. *Journal of Banking & Finance* 17 (2–3): 515–530.
Safiullah, M., and A. Shamsuddin. 2019. Risk-adjusted efficiency and corporate governance: Evidence from Islamic and conventional banks. *Journal of Corporate Finance* 55: 105–140.
Sharma, V. 2011. Independent directors and the propensity to pay dividends. *Journal of Corporate Finance* 17 (4): 1001–1015.
Shivdasani, A. 1993. Board composition, ownership structure, and hostile takeovers. *Journal of Accounting and Economics* 16 (1–3): 167–198.
Shivdasani, A., and D. Yermack. 1999. CEO involvement in the selection of new board members: An empirical analysis. *The Journal of Finance* 54 (5): 1829–1853.
Sierra, G.E., E. Talmor, and J.S. Wallace. 2006. An examination of multiple governance forces within bank holding companies. *Journal of Financial Services Research* 29 (2): 105–123.
Toufik, B.B. 2015. The Role of Shari ah Supervisory Board (SSB) in Ensuring Good Corporate Governance Practice in Islamic Banks. *International Journal of Contemporary Applied Sciences* 2 (2): 109–118.
Trinh, V.Q., M. Elnahass, and A. Salama. 2021. Board busyness and new insights into alternative bank dividends models. *Review of Quantitative Finance and Accounting* 56 (4): 1289–1328.
Vafeas, N. 1999. Board meeting frequency and firm performance. *Journal of Financial Economics* 53 (1): 113–142.
Williamson, O.E. 1984. Corporate governance. *The Yale Law Journal* 93: 1197.
Wintoki, M.B., J.S. Linck, and J.M. Netter. 2012. Endogeneity and the dynamics of internal corporate governance. *Journal of Financial Economics* 105 (3): 581–606.
Zajac, E.J., and J.D. Westphal 1996, August. Director reputation, CEO/Board power, and the dynamics of board interlocks. In *Academy of Management Proceedings* (Vol. 1996, No. 1, pp. 254–258). Briarcliff Manor, NY 10510: Academy of Management.
Zhang, E.J. 2016. *Preoccupied independent directors*. Working paper, UNSW Business School.

Chapter 4
Dual Banking System: Conventional and Islamic Banks

4.1 Fundamentals of Islamic Banking Model

The Key Pillar of Islamic banks is basically the prohibition of interest. Thus, their core function is profit-loss sharing (PLS) paradigm that financial transactions ideally reflect a symmetrical risk-return distribution among parties (e.g., El-Hawary et al. 2007; Askari et al. 2010; Saeed and Izzeldin 2016; Elnahass et al. 2018).

4.1.1 What Is the PLS Paradigm?

Due to the prohibition of charging interest in Islamic banking, depositors are recognised as investment account holders (IAHs). IAHs are those who enter into *equity-based* investment contracts with the bank. Under these arrangements, banks can *share* in profits, while losses are borne by the investment account holders (Elnahass et al. 2018).

4.1.2 What Are Islamic Banks?

Islamic banks refer to businesses operating similarly to equity-based firms that *depositors are treated as investors rather than creditors* (Khan and Mirakhor 1989; Aysan et al. 2016). Deposits in this banking system could be broadly classified into two accounts: current (or demand) deposit and profit sharing investment accounts (Grais and Pellegrini 2006; Van Greuning and Iqbal 2008). Based on the Amanah and Wadiah principle:

V. Quang Trinh, *Fundamentals of Board Busyness and Corporate Governance*, Contributions to Management Science,
https://doi.org/10.1007/978-3-030-89228-9_4

(i) *Current deposit account:* is similar to those of traditional (conventional) banks (Van Greuning and Iqbal 2008).
(ii) *Profit sharing investment account:* based on a Mudaraba contract, it is considered as the main distinguishing characteristics (Archer and Karim 2009) that IAHs or quasi-equity holders do not have any participations in bank management governance or in the direct monitoring of entrepreneurs (Athari et al. 2016). According to Greuning and Iqbal (2008), investment accounts comprise of two categories which are *unrestricted* and *restricted* investment accounts. Unlike restricted accounts, depositors of unrestricted accounts allow managers of Islamic banks to invest in any Shari'ah compliant investment.

Islamic banks place their funds in Shari'ah compliant investment pools and distribute profits and losses based on a predetermined PLS ratio. The sources of those funds can come from either shareholders or depositors who are also called customers who share risk and return with shareholders (Athari et al. 2016).

From the standpoint of Shari'ah rulings,[1] the relation in nature between Islamic banking and those shareholders/depositors will be based on an agreement between the fund owners and the fund managers.[2] The former must bear the financial loss entirely if the loss is not due to latter's negligence.

According to Islamic legislation, some crucial conditions may be stipulated in the contracts between them; for instance, the net profits earned are equally distributed between shareholders and depositors which is based on the balance as well as duration of the investment. The excess amount of profit remaining after deducting any relevant expenses (e.g., reserves and provisions[3]) from revenues is defined by Shari'ah as profit. Meanwhile, the natural relation between shareholders and depositors would be built upon on the shareholding company which mainly attributes to such relation that shareholders might have equal rights and claims to the company the income or loss upon on the level of participation. However, shareholders can agree with a higher income of a partner (than his/her original share) as a compensation for additional efforts and services.

From a practical perspective, the displaced commercial risk can be arisen when shareholders are willing to offer a sacrifice on their income to pay for the bank depositors with an aim to maintain the firm reputation and competitiveness (Archer and Karim 2006). Islamic banks' shareholders, known as bank legal owners, can appoint the board of directors who play crucial and direct role in overlooking the bank strategies, management team, firm control and operations.

[1]Two key principles in Shari'ah law include Justice and Equity which ensure that none of parties involved in an activity is being exploited (Malkawi 2013).

[2]These managers should have the knowledge and expertise in the area of business (Emirates Islamic Bank 2009). They charge management fees against the service rendered.

[3]Except for the case of a restricted investment account which is treated as off-balance sheet items. In such case, no reserves and provisions are deducted.

4.2 Practice of Shari'ah Governance Framework

As discussed earlier, the separation of ownership and control in modern organisations is the origin of agency conflicts (Jensen and Meckling 1976). Such divergence involves agency costs, arise because of the opportunities for conflict of interest, and laid upon the shareholders (the principals) when managers (the agents) act in their personal interests at the expense of those of principals (Fama and Jensen 1983). As such, the principals try, through governance mechanisms, to minimise these costs and protect their interests.

Agency relationships and governance sittings in Islamic banking are unique and more complex as the nature of their operations distinguishes them from conventional counterparts and widens the issue of separation of ownership and control underlying the agency theory (Safieddine 2009). Governance in Islam, albeit similar to the Anglo-American model, is always perceived as being more strengthened with an additional layer of monitoring or supervision in the form of religious or ethical boards (Elnahass et al. 2014; Mollah and Zaman 2015; Abdelsalam et al. 2016)—the so-called Shari'ah Supervisory Board (SSB). The SSB is an independent body of Islamic banks which is entrusted with directing, reviewing, and supervising the operations and transactions of this bank type for the purpose of Shari'ah/Islamic compliance (Malkawi 2013).

4.2.1 *What Is the Shari'ah Governance?*

Shari'ah governance[4] is defined as a set of institutional arrangements which is associated with the direction, management, governance and control of the SSB (Malkawi 2013). It can be viewed as one of the unique kinds of governance in financial architecture because of the following reasons:

- It is concerned with the religious aspects of the overall operations of Islamic banking system in comparison with traditional concept of corporate governance in conventional banking (Malkawi 2013).
- It concerns the management, establishment, as well as affairs of the Shari'ah board.

The Shari'ah board is always seen as being a key player in ensuring good Shari'ah governance (Choudhury and Alam 2013; Alnasser and Muhammed 2012). However, the establishment of the SSB is relatively new in the Islamic banking model (Malkawi 2013).

---

[4]Islamic Financial Service Board (IFSB) and the Accounting and Auditing Organizations for Islamic Financial Institutions (AAOIFI) are two main of several independent international entities which are established to support the Islamic financial industry with regard to Shari'ah governance (see Malkawi 2013)

- The organising of the SSB began in 1976 when the Faisal Islamic Bank of Egypt was established. This bank thus was the first one which has the SSB as formal religious board in the corporate governance (see Malkawi 2013). This practice then was followed by several banks including Jordan Islamic Bank and Faisal Islamic Bank of Sudan (1978), the Kuwait Finance House (1979), the Bank Islam Malaysia Berhad (1983), and the Dubai Islamic Bank (1999). As of today, most of Islamic banks have established their own SSB.
- The SSB has profound influence on the day-to-day practice of finance in providing both consultative and supervisory services to the Islamic banks (Mollah et al. 2017). Therefore, they provide an additional check and should add value to this bank type (Mollah and Zaman 2015).
- The SSB members endeavour to respond to any issues for a transaction or product conformation with the Shari'ah and offer advice and recommendations to the board of directors (Kettell 2011; Mollah and Zaman 2015).
- The SSB should seek enhancing the Islamic banking knowledge among the employees (Alnasser and Muhammed 2012).
- The SSB review bank activities and processes, supervise its development of Islamic financial products and services, endorse and validate relevant documentations, as well as the internal policies and manuals and marketing advertisements (Alnasser and Muhammed 2012), and determine the Shari'ah compliance of these products and the investments (Choudhury and Alam 2013; Elnahass et al. 2014).
- SSB members act as investigators in carrying their own independent audit to certify that nothing relating to any of the bank's operations involve any element prohibited by Shari'ah (Safieddine 2009). The SSB then issues an independent report to certify that all financial transactions comply with Shari'ah principles. This report is often an integral part of the annual report of the Islamic bank (Grais and Pellegrini 2006).

In brief, the main roles of the SSB might normally involve in three different areas including the issuance of fatawa[5] (a non-binding advisory opinion to an individual questioner in connection with ongoing human affairs) via collective ijtihad[6] (use of independent reasoning by qualified scholars to obtain legal rules), internal supervision/control mechanism (raqabah), and internal audit (mutabaah) (Malkawi 2013).

Due to the rapid growth of Islamic banking sector, along with the global banking crisis 2007–2009, the SSB requires an enhanced governance framework. Specifically, in carrying out its activities and fulfilling the imperative tasks, this board needs to have a clear framework/structure to ensure its independence and effectiveness. The presence of SSB tends to play a catalytic role in promoting public acceptance for this banking industry. In other words, effective SSB is vital to strengthen the creditability of the Islamic banks. In contrast, the failure of providing an effective

[5]It covers issues of mosques, intergenerational transmission of property, and marriage of children, and banking operations and interest (Malkawi 2013).

[6]It is one of the sources of Islamic law. It meaning is reasoning and strict legal analogy (Malkawi 2013).

SSB is likely to inevitably result in serious disruptions in the financial market which in turn, leads to dire consequences for the Islamic banking and finance sector (Malkawi 2013).

In Islamic banks, the agents are required to adhere to Islamic principles of Shari'ah in fulfilling their missions to maximise shareholders' wealth (Safieddine 2009). The stakeholders' interest in Islamic banks may extend beyond the financial interest to ethical and religious values (Alnasser and Muhammed 2012). The SSB is constrainedly based in its supervisory objectives and monitoring operations on Shari'ah (Islamic law) principles (Haniffa and Hudaib 2007; Hassan et al. 2003).

Any divergence by Islamic banks' agents from placing all supplied funds in Shari'ah-compliant investments creates an additional source of agency problems (Safieddine 2009). Such Islamic doctrines include prohibiting charging of and giving interest or usury, also commonly called '*riba*' in Islamic discourse, as it exemplifies both the earning of money on money via a predetermined rate on a deposit or loan and a social injustice (Gambling and Karim 1986), forbidding uncertainty or speculation (*gharar*) (Kettell 2011), curbing engagement in aggressive lending and major risk-taking activities (Beck et al. 2013; Mollah and Zaman 2015), placing an embargo on financing of activities regarded as harmful to society and, therefore, conflict with ethics and moral values (e.g., gambling and alcohol) (Kettell 2011), and practicing equitable distribution of the financial rewards (i.e., profit-sharing—*mudaraba*) and risks of investments (i.e., partnership or the profit-and-loss sharing—*musharaka*) (Bashir 1983; Dar and Presley 2000). Within these Islamic norms, Islamic financial products and services are designed.

In practice, notable governance challenges encounter SSBs roles (Grais and Pellegrini 2006) and would relatively affect their moral responsibility. Members of this board are appointed by shareholders at the Annual General Meeting (AGM) or by the board of directors. The International Association of Islamic Bank points out that Shari'ah members must not be recruited by the bank and especially should not subject to the authority of the board of directors (Rammal 2006). The purpose of this is to ensure freedom and independence of the SSB. However, in many cases, the appointments of the SSB made by the AGM are based on the recommendation by the board of directors. If so, the SSB members are allowed to attend the board of directors' meetings to discuss the religious aspects of the board of directors' decisions (see Malkawi 2013).

In practice, the board of directors in numerous Islamic banks can also directly appoint Shari'ah scholars, as in Pakistan, Jordan, Malaysia, etc. This is evidenced by the survey of International Institute of Islamic Thought, with 80 per cent of SSB appointments made by the board of directors. Because the assumption of SSB independence could only be guaranteed if the appointments of SSB members are made by AGM, practitioners claim that this assumption is not truly convincing as the practice of appointments in fact varies among the Islamic banks. Even if the appointments are made by the AGM, the board of directors may still influence shareholders during recruitment process (Malkawi 2013).

SSB members will receive the remunerations from the Islamic bank where they are serving, and the board of directors has power to fix and approve such remuneration (Rammal 2006; Gooden 2001; Malkawi 2013). Therefore, some loyalty to managers/banks/board of directors who proposed them in the first place is expected (see Hart 1995). This may create a potential conflict of interest (Rammal 2006). Moreover, their employment status as both advisors and supervisors also breed a financial stake in the bank. This further generates agency costs because of the opportunities for compromised independence and a potential conflict of interest.

The bank's top managers may use their power to gain more accredited opinions to maximise their own self-interest (Jensen and Meckling 1976; Fama 1980), producing what is commonly referred to as "fatwa (religious verdict) shopping" (Grais and Pellegrini 2006), or ex ante Shari'ah audit (Alnasser and Muhammed 2012). Accordingly, in some Islamic financial institutions, SSB members can be perceived as merely serving as "window dressing".

SSB members should not only be knowledgeable in Islamic commercial jurisprudence. They should also be equipped with relevant expertise in modern business disciplines, economic developments, and accounting and financial practices and armed with adequate training and continuing education (Malkawi 2013). In practice, very few religious scholars are well educated, trained, and highly experienced in disciplines of Shari'ah law and finance (Alnasser and Muhammed 2012). Bearing in mind also the fact that audit committees are expected to monitor managers' financial reporting, their role tends to be quite limited among Islamic banks, showing increasing agency problems (Safieddine 2009).

Furthermore, a survey by Mollah and Zaman (2015) documents that Islamic banks only review of the SSB qualifications and expertise without assessing the board performance throughout their employment. The responses from this survey were mixed regarding SSB training and understanding of internal controls and risk management processes.

More importantly, however, is the fact that a limited number of the most prominent and respected scholars control the Islamic banking industry and sit on multiple SSBs on a part-time basis (Khalaf 2007; Alnasser and Muhammed 2012; Mollah and Zaman 2015). Because there are not many scholars qualified in both Shari'ah law and finance, there is an unusual high concentration of positions in very few hands (Khalaf 2007). Many of these scholars are highly regarded with their opinions (i.e., having reputational capital) and advise many financial organisations at the same time, and hence, overworked with multiple duties (Al-Rai 2010).

In addition, there exists several problems related to the selection criteria and qualifications of SSB members amongst Islamic banks. Their education is not properly regulated and coordinated, and particularly, no specific curricula for them are established (McMillen 2006). These lead to a reduction in the SSB roles' effectiveness, especially in providing solid and concrete fatawa rulings that require professional skills/knowledge/training and expertise in Shari'ah (Malkawi 2013).

Furthermore, as the industry grows rapidly, the efficacy of "too-busy" SSB members who are overcommitted has been called into question. Under this tremendous growth, one must worry that the number of potential conflicting fatawa among SSB members of the different SSB will increase (Malkawi 2013). It is thus imperative to examine knowledge, experience, skills and time/efforts of those Shari'ah scholars. Additionally, the SSB normally meets weekly, monthly, semi-annually, quarterly, or annually, depending on the need of Islamic banks (Malkawi 2013). This signifies the huge number of meetings of several Shari'ah scholars which makes them spend lots of their time and efforts to fully get involve in their banks where they are working for.

Additional concerns could also be raised whether scholars are part of competing banks or if they must regulate the bank of which they are a part (Khalaf 2007). Such scarcity and "busyness" of SSB members could undermine stakeholders' confidence in the credibility of their assessments. Hence, while theory suggests that the additional layer of monitoring through SSBs can restrain excessive risk-taking (e.g., Elnahass et al. 2014; Abdelsalam et al. 2016), the SSB monitoring effectiveness depends on the time and efforts allocated by its individual members. This represents an ultimate indicator of the activity level exercised by its members in advising and supervising the board of directors.

Academics and practitioners, both, contend that it is essential to have a legal provision that states clearly restrictions on serving multiple SSBs of Islamic banks at the same time, which can avoid any perception of conflict of interest (Akhtar 2007; Malkawi 2013). Such policy can ensure full-time availability of the SSB to provide advisory and supervisory services to the Islamic banks more effectively. A well-functioning SSB, working in concert with the regular board of directors, routines executive and other operational committees, is necessary to ensure that the noble goals of Islamic banking are achieved in practice.

As a result of rapid expansion of Islamic banking and finance, along with the increasing number of SSB, the issues of competency of SSB members as well as of interest's conflict require a legal framework regulating the SSB qualifications and ability of sitting on multiple boards (see Malkawi 2013).

4.3 Differences Between Islamic and Conventional Banks

Based on the fundamental principles of Islamic banks, this book suggests five main aspects that differentiate Islamic banking model (i.e., Shari'ah compliant finance) from their conventional counterparts (see Beck et al. 2013; Abdelsalam et al. 2016). They include:

1. *Business model and investment modes*
2. *Constraints on finance model and prohibited activities*
3. *Agency conflicts*
4. *Corporate governance mechanism*
5. *Dividend pay-out model*

These dissimilarities appear to be originated from the specific codes of behaviour in the Muslim religion and the distinctive character of this kind of bank (Abedifar et al. 2013; Mollah and Zaman 2015). See Fig. 4.1.

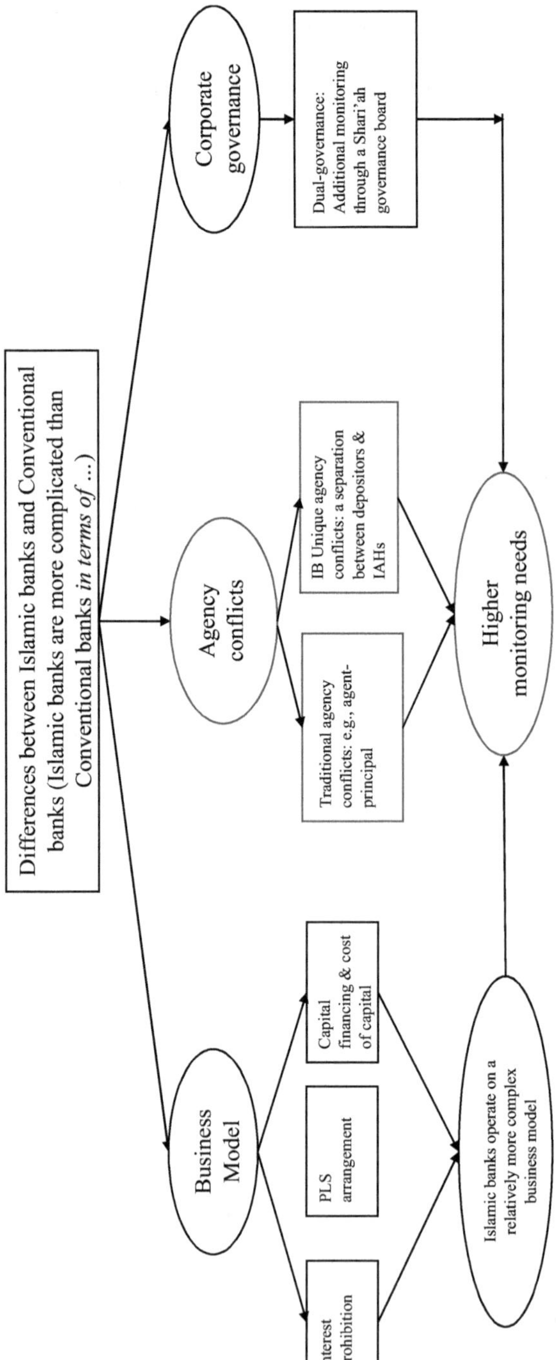

Fig. 4.1 A Comparison between Islamic and conventional bank. Source: author (based on previous studies)

4.3.1 Business Model and Investment Modes: Risk-Transfer Model (Conventional Banks) vs Profit-Loss Sharing Paradigm (Islamic Banks)

Like their conventional counterparts, Islamic banks are still engaged in the activities of dealing in money such as collection of deposits, lending, and investing (Malkawi 2013). However, whilst Conventional banks are directly involved in lending and borrowing business and act only as the moneylender, Islamic banks work on trading and investments model and not lend the money directly (Elnahass et al. 2018).

What distinguishes Islamic banks from Conventional banks is that their dealings with depositors will be based on profit-loss sharing (i.e., PLS) paradigm rather than a fixed pre-determined interest, signifying a fiduciary role for those Islamic banks where it might be considered to be dealing in trust money (Malkawi 2013; Mallin et al. 2014; Saeed and Izzeldin 2016). Islamic banks operated on a PLS financing mode in which contracts between the banks and their depositors (i.e., investment account holders, IAHs) are commonly equity-based, which implies that all transactions are backed by real economic activities linked to tangible assets (Elnahass et al. 2018).

In trading by the PLS paradigm, Islamic banks are, in general, considered as more financially stable than Conventional banks (Abedifar et al. 2013; Beck et al. 2013). In order for Islamic banks and their customers to comply with Islamic rulings, specific products and services have been introduced and developed over the past decades which can avoid the concept of interest and imply a certain degree of risk-sharing (Beck et al. 2013).

Despite Islamic banks are seen as a constrained banking model, their PLS finance mode is likely to allow higher discretion in the administration of investment accounts as well as financial reporting (Mills and Presley 1999) where tighten monitoring of financial reporting from investors (i.e., IAHs), in the absence of direct scrutinising, tends to be anticipated. Such enhanced scrutinising suggests that adverse selection and moral hazard might be less likely to be occurred (Beck et al. 2013).

4.3.2 Constraints on Finance Model and Prohibited Activities: Interest-Based Structure (Conventional Banks) vs Non-interest-Based Structure (Islamic Banks)

In principle, unlike the conventional banking system with the interest-based structure, Islamic banks survive under the strict Shari'ah governing framework having Shari'ah guidelines and a SSB which approves all transactions, activities and products in line with Islamic principles (Beck et al. 2013).

To contribute to the achievement of social justice, Islamic banks are expected to discard the interest-based financial system of Conventional banks. They prohibit the interest payment and their transactions must commit the principles of religion (Obaidullah 2005; Iqbal and Llewellyn 2002; Zaher and Hassan 2001). They, therefore, replace conventional financial contracts (time deposits, debt financing and lease financing) by other specific forms of financial contracts (mark-up financing (murabaha) and profit-sharing financing (mudaraba and musharaka) (Mollah et al. 2017; Farook et al. 2012; Khediri et al. 2015).

Those finance modes prevent excess uncertainty (Gharar), speculations (Maysir) and financing on illicit sectors (i.e., weapons, drugs, alcohol and pork) but increase the sharing of profit, loss and risks among stakeholders (Abdelsalam et al. 2016; Beck et al. 2013), hence, affect IB's performance including risk, stability and efficiency (Abedifar et al. 2013; Beck et al. 2013).

In addition, Shari'ah-compliant funding of Islamic banks appears to restrict them to borrow from international financial markets (Elnahass et al. 2018). PLS finance mode used by Islamic banks is related to a limited use of hedging instruments (Trinh et al. 2021).

Due to the complexities of the Islamic products and the transaction mechanism involved, Islamic banking investments tend to be more risky than conventional banking investments (Olson and Zoubi 2008; Abedifar et al. 2013). The credit risk of Islamic banks can be increased because the PLS does not require any collateral or guarantees (Mollah et al. 2017). It is, therefore, expected that relatively compared to Conventional banks, Islamic banks should apply a credit-risk management strategy which features greater loan loss reserves and greater regulatory capital ratios, but lower asset utilisation (Elnahass et al. 2018).

As regards next three other aspects, the above key differences may lead to the dissimilarities between the two bank types in terms of agency conflicts, corporate governance mechanism (Abdelsalam et al. 2016), and dividend pay-out model. See Fig. 4.1 below.

4.3.3 Agency Conflicts: More Complex Agency Conflicts of Islamic Bank than Conventional

Islamic banks are widely known as a special bank type having a unique agency relationship which seems to be more complicated than that of Conventional banks (Safieddine 2009; Mallin et al. 2014). They often offer diversified activities and relations among stakeholders including depositors, banks and investors. Most of these stakeholders are particularly concerned that whether their money is employed in a Shari'ah-compliant manner or not (Chapra and Ahmed 2002).

Islamic banks agency conflicts are expected to be more complex than those of Conventional banks that include two main conflicts: traditional and Islamic banks' unique conflict. Besides traditional conflicts (agent-principal) that both types of banks (Islamic banks and Conventional banks) might face (Fama and Jensen 1983; Jensen and Smith 1985; Bowie and Freeman 1992; La Porta et al. 1999), Islamic banks must face additional conflict between managers and depositors leading to higher agency costs and greater legal liability for executives within Islamic banks (Abdelsalam et al. 2016). This is in line with more effective competition and deposit insurance in Conventional banks and the unique institutional settings of Islamic banks (Nienhaus 2007; Archer and Karim 2009).

For example, managers of Islamic banks typically based on the benchmark rate of return of the Conventional banks to set profit sharing ratios. This rate is often lower than the risk-identical return rate for Conventional banks. Both managers and shareholders in Islamic banks can increase their profit share to exploit investment account holders (IAHs) who seems not to be fully aware of potential risks. Therefore, the determination of these profit-loss sharing rates should incur the fundamental conflicts (Nienhaus 2007).

Using PLS financing methods (hybrid equity and debt financing) in Islamic banks encourages managers to employ funds of quasi-equity holders for their private interests (Bacha 1996). They can easily mitigate profits by increasing accrued costs, but an increase in private benefits and perks is likely to be more than the decrease in their share of profits. IAHs do not have governance rights to control management behaviour and decisions, they thus mainly reply on "vicarious monitoring" by shareholders (Archer et al. 1998).

However, if such "vicarious monitoring" is not effective, the conflicts between IAHs and shareholders are more likely (Archer and Karim 2002). Given such unique governance structure, both bank managers and shareholders might have stronger incentives to expropriate IAHs funds. Consequently, Islamic banks must face more significant adverse selection and moral hazard problems in both sides of the balance sheet (Nienhaus 2007; Athari et al. 2016).

Moreover, Islamic banks might also face increased agency costs on both sides of their balance sheet, in respect of depositors who investing their wealth in firm loans/assets and where Islamic banks perform as their agent, and on the asset side where borrowers play an agent role who employ money of depositors to invest (Beck et al. 2013). A signed debt contract between the bank and depositors/borrowers with deterministic (Diamond 1984) and stochastic monitoring (Townsend 1979) is considered as optimal choice for Islamic banks with the numerous numbers of savers and entrepreneurs.

Nonetheless, Islamic banks obviously must face maturity mismatch between deposits, demandable on sight and long-run loans which has high probability leading to firm runs and default (Diamond and Dybvig 1983). As a result, Islamic banks are argued to be face double agency problems: with reference to depositors who might monitor bank activities, encouraging the bank in turn monitor borrowers whilst interference of the government, for example deposit insurance which gives a misleading of such equipoise (Diamond and Rajan 2001).

Prominently, while the concept of interest is considered as the return on capital of Conventional banks, receipts and payments of interest is prohibited within Islamic banks. Therefore, depositors in Islamic banks are contracted as IAHs by an equity-based investment contract (Mudarabah). This leads to the comingling between IAHs and Shareholders' fund resulting in the return comingling; and therefore, potential agency conflict problem might be risen in Islamic banks between protection of IAHs' rights and shareholders which have unsolved (Claessens 2006).

Profit from investments are expected to share between the IAHs and the Islamic bank upon on mutually agreement between them about proportion. Nonetheless, the IAHs must completely bear all losses from investments, except for the case of misconducting or negligence from the bank (Belal et al. 2015; Aggarwal and Yousef 2000).

Unfortunately, in practice, most of Islamic banks do not entitle directly monitor their investment by having representatives seating in board of directors resulting in higher agency costs and the IAHs' risk of exploitation by firm executives (Archer and Karim 2002). Furthermore, the difference between Islamic banks' PLS mechanism and Conventional bank's traditional mechanism is about employing equity financing and risk sharing compared to debt financing and risk transference respectively (Hasan and Dridi 2011; Beck et al. 2013).

Adverse selection and moral hazard problems are expected to be arise more often in the PLS mechanism of Islamic banks than traditional mechanism of their conventional counterparts (Mollah et al. 2017). However, the presence of SSB in Islamic banks, in case that it can fully fulfil its tasks, are argued to support higher public trust and confidence of IAH who have no representation in the board of directors and, thus, the moral hazard risks are predicted to be less.

4.3.4 Corporate Governance Mechanism: More Complex Corporate Governance Mechanism of Islamic than Conventional Banks

The relationships within Conventional banks are enclosed to private banking services for key customers whilst close relationships in Islamic banks mainly derive from shared values, trust and mutual respect (Mollah et al. 2017). Hence, several types of Islamic banks' risks should be diminished by alleviating transaction costs and lessening agency conflicts through observing by depositors rather than interferences of government authorities (i.e., deposit insurance) (Beck et al. 2013).

However, the complexities of Islamic banks as well as Shari'ah compliance administration also suggests additional risks for Islamic banks, especially increased credit risk as the profit and loss sharing mode of financing of Islamic banks does not have need of guarantees (Mollah et al. 2017). Islamic banks differ, therefore, fundamentally from secular institutions offering conventional financial services—Conventional banks.

In Conventional banks, the board of directors tends to define appropriate corporate governance and practices for its own work (Shibani and De Fuentes 2017).

Therefore, they do not have the religious preoccupations or an extra layer of governance: the SSB (Kettell 2011; Mollah et al. 2017).

Contrast to this "single-layer" governance structure of Conventional banks, which typically includes the board of directors and executive/board subcommittees, the "multi-layer" governance of Islamic banks comprises of board of directors, extended religious board namely SSB, and executive/board subcommittees (Mollah and Zaman 2015).

In other words, the corporate governance of Islamic financial institutions are subject to a multi-level governance system where stakeholders are more concerned with the religious elements in the governance structure, given the SSB a distinguishing feature of those Islamic business organisations (Quttainah et al. 2013). Indeed, besides the main responsibilities of execution, protecting the shareholders' interest and maximising their value, the board of directors in Islamic banks has additional functions related to the introduction of comprehensive policies, processes, and infrastructure to ensure that all activities/transactions/policies of Islamic banks are compliance with Shari'ah law, and establish an appropriate Shari'ah governance framework. Thus, the functional role of the Islamic banks must be applied via the Shari'ah rulings.

Meanwhile, the role of the Shareholders is to be active participants and conscious stakeholders in the process of decision-making and policy framework by taking into account all interests of stakeholders (i.e., board of directors, SSB, shareholders and other stakeholders) rather than maximising profit alone (Hasan 2009). There are two corporate governance layers in Islamic banking system:

- *SSB layer*: The extended layer of Islamic banking governance (SSB) is referred as "supra authority". It protects Islamic Community and focuses on the compliance of the ethos of Shari'ah on firm's activities and transactions, monitors and controls the board of directors and executive management team to ensure that they only execute the ex-ante approved products and services compliance to Shari'ah law as well as help the staffs in Islamic banks to adhere the morality principles rather than personal interests and greed (Beekun and Badawi 2005; Shibani and De Fuentes 2017). SSB, therefore, should restrain board of directors and managers from their aggressive lending, risk-taking and unethical behaviours (Mollah and Zaman 2015).
- *Board of directors layer*: the board of directors enforces the authority of the SSB to perform their either supervisory or advisory roles, or both (Mollah et al. 2017).

Shari'ah requirements, therefore, lead to unique agency relations of Islamic banks, especially as financial turmoil can be produced by the Shari'ah non-compliance risk (Safieddine 2009). Thus, corporate governance system of Islamic banks is more complicated than that of Conventional banks to control for those agency conflicts (Lewis 2008).

Undoubtedly, the "single-layer" governance mechanism of Conventional banks suggests that their board of directors is more independent in its decision-making process than in Islamic counterparts with "multi-layer" governance (Alnasser and Muhammed 2012; Mollah and Zaman 2015; Mollah et al. 2017).

4.3.5 Dividend Pay-out Model: More Complex Dividend Pay-out Model of Islamic Bank than Conventional

As discussed previously, the key feature differentiating Islamic from conventional financial intermediaries is the additional monitoring through a Shari'ah governance board, and the dominance of Islamic principles over the business model (i.e., the prohibition of interests and of speculative and uncertain trading activities). Under the conventional banking finance paradigm, a bank is likely to shift credit risk to the depositors under an interest-based contractual arrangement (Safiullah and Shamsuddin 2019). Contrarily, as per Shari'ah guidelines, Islamic banks are expected to perform their intermediation functions through PLS contractual agreements between the banks, depositors and IAHs (Farag et al. 2018).

According to the PLS paradigm, entrepreneurs share their profits and losses with Islamic banks according to a pre-determined ratio. Islamic banks pool all profits and losses from different investments and share the profits with depositors of funds taking into account the relative contributions of capital and equity and the investment deposits (Olson and Zoubi 2008). A proportion of the remaining earned profits is used to pay dividends to equity holders, for which dividends on common equity is discretionarily allocated and distributed by the bank managers (Khan and Mirakhor 1989).

The Islamic bank dividend model under this PLS paradigm indicates substantial differences in the distribution principles, the extent of flexibility of pay-outs and the mechanics and techniques when compared to the conventional banking dividend model (e.g., Ayub 2007; Beck et al. 2013; Athari et al. 2016). This book follows the study of Trinh et al. (2021) to summarise these key differences in Table 4.1. These differences are expected to influence the governance monitoring effectiveness of both bank types and the overall levels of dividend pay-outs.

First, a pay-out policy in an Islamic bank is likely to be less flexible than that of a Conventional bank. While the dividend distribution decisions of the former are significantly affected by their challenges in managing liquidity and accessing short-term borrowings from outside sources (Beck et al. 2013; Elnahass et al. 2014), the latter has better liquidity opportunities promoted by their ease and quick access to external market sources and the availability of alternative instruments to raise funds such as hedging and derivatives (Bitar et al. 2017; Deng et al. 2017). Islamic banks, therefore, are likely to hold greater capital buffers to mitigate their liquidity challenges as well as preserve their regulatory capital ratios. The existence of limited sources of finance, such as the issuance of Islamic bonds, to enhance the liquidity and capital position leads to substantial restrictions imposed on the bank business model and dividends strategies (Elnahass et al. 2014). As a result, Conventional banks are better positioned to offer more frequent pay-outs of dividends at higher rates when compared to Islamic banking (Athari et al. 2016).

Second, Islamic banks encounter additional challenges related to their actual (Shari'ah) profit determination compared to Conventional banks. Under the constrained dividends model, any fraction of earnings which are generated from

Table 4.1 A comparison between Islamic and conventional bank dividend model

Aspects	Islamic banking dividends model	Conventional banking dividends model
Shari'ah compliance and PLS principle is applied	*Yes*	*None*
Rate of return on deposits	*Uncertain, not guaranteed*	*Certain and guaranteed*
Motives of pay-outs	Preferences of both investors (shareholders) and depositors	Preference of investors (shareholders)
Conflicts between depositors and shareholders towards dividend pay-outs ratio for the latter	*High*	*Low*
Depositors' return is linked to the return on assets	*Yes*	*No*
Banks' pooling of depositors' funds to provide depositors with professional investment management	*Yes*	*No*
Process Activeness	*High.* Profit distribution is a more active process involving a nexus of contracts between the bank, depositors and shareholders. Hence, the profit distribution of Islamic banks is agreement among such three parties including depositors.	*Low.* Depositors will receive interest payment from the banks. Interests paid for depositors are treated as expenses when calculating net profits and dividends for shareholders. Hence, the profit distribution of conventional banks is only an agreement between shareholders and the bank.
Complexity of pay-outs mechanics and techniques	*High.* Dividend decision subjects to the interaction between PSIA and dividend distributions. It depends much on the effectiveness of profit distribution among parties under the PLS arrangements.	*Low.* Dividend decisions are not subject to the interaction between PSIA and dividend distributions; however, they are associated with current profitability, future growth opportunities, and optimal capital budget and equity amount needed to finance the optimal budget through retained earnings.
Difficulties in pay-outs	*High.* It is difficult to determine the actual (Shari'ah) profits for any financial year because some investment projects may not be finished before the end of the accounting year. In addition, Islamic banks cannot use all the available fund to undertake investment activities which challenges their profit/dividend distribution.	*Low.* Interest amounts are treated as expenses which are paid to depositors. Such expenses do not depend on the completion of investments and conventional banks can pool and employ all available capital. Net profits (after all expenses) will be distributed to shareholders according to the shareholding percentages.

(continued)

Table 4.1 (continued)

Aspects	Islamic banking dividends model	Conventional banking dividends model
Flexibility of pay-outs policy	*Low.* Dividend decisions appear to be significantly affected by Islamic banks' challenges in managing liquidity and accessing Shari'ah short-term borrowings from outside sources.	*High.* Higher liquidity position as they enable quicker access to external market sources and the use of hedging and financial instruments.
Agency conflicts arise during pay-outs process	*High.* The conflicts occur when managers, depositors and shareholders disagree about the profit distribution. Managers have more opportunities engage in discretionary acts comprising of controlling and managing dividend policy.	*Low.* The conflicts occur only when managers and shareholders disagree about the profit distribution. This lowers opportunities for bank managers' to engage in discretionary acts, relative to Islamic banks.
Prediction for the Levels of pay-outs	*Low*	*High*

Source: Trinh et al. (2021)

investments that do not comply with the Islamic principles cannot be distributed to shareholders or used to acquire assets (Safiullah and Shamsuddin 2019). Given that an Islamic bank's contracts should, in principle, be backed by underlying assets or investment activity, in many occasions it is too complex to determine the estimated profits when some projects have not yet been realised before the end of the fiscal period. This can have implications on the bank's dividends pay-outs. Also, unlike their conventional counterparts, Islamic banks cannot employ all the capital available to undertake investment opportunities, either because the regulations do not allow them, or because the capital available for investment is higher than the Islamic banks' investment portfolio (Ahmed 1996).

However, such related complexities and issues are not raised in a Conventional bank business model as Islamic rulings will not constrain its distributable profits. Depositors in this bank type obtain their returns in the form of regular/composite interest payments which are treated as expenses when Conventional banks compute their net profits and dividends for shareholders. As such, an important difference between Islamic banks and Conventional banks in this respect is the shift in treating returns payable to depositors as a distribution of shared profits and not an expense (Alhabshi 2002; Saeed and Izzeldin 2016). Moreover, in contrast to Islamic banks, the interest expenses paid for depositors in Conventional banks should be independent of the completion of investment projects. These banks, hence, may have lower difficulties of calculating profits distributable for shareholders. Accordingly, the Islamic bank financial structure of a dividend-based model differs from Conventional banks (Schaik 2001; Safiullah and Shamsuddin 2019), which may, in turn, lead to different pay-out levels between the two bank types.

Third, with the restrictions imposed on the Islamic bank dividends model, which must comply with the Shari'ah principles, profit distributions by Islamic banks reflect an active process involving a nexus of contracts between the bank, depositors and equity holders (Schaik 2001; Alhabshi 2002; Safiullah and Shamsuddin 2019). Thereby, the profit and dividend pay-out decisions of Islamic banks are associated with an agreement among these three parties. In other words, the basis and manner of profit distributions could change in future and are subject to the contract agreement among parties. This adds to the main structural differences in the distribution motives of Islamic banks relative to their conventional counterparts. The pay-outs decisions by Islamic banks' managers are ultimately driven by the preferences of both investors and depositors. In contrast, a sound distribution policy in Conventional banks depends solely and mainly on the preference of investors (shareholders) to enhance the bank market value (Al-Hunnayan and Hashem 2011). As such, compared to Conventional banks, additional monitoring costs imposed on Islamic banks might be needed to avoid disappointing the investors/depositors.

Finally, the mechanics and techniques of Islamic bank dividend distributions are likely to be more complicated than those of Islamic banks (Athari et al. 2016). A survey by Al-Hunnayan and Hashem (2011) defines a commonly used dividend model in an Islamic bank and summarises its key structures based on four steps; (i) revenues and expenses allocation; (ii) reserves and provisions deductions; (iii) distributions for profit and loss saving and investment accounts (PSIA); and (iv) distribute dividends. This is re-supported by the study of Trinh et al. (2021). At each step of this pay-out process, there are potential variations in the practices of Islamic banks. Moreover, under the PLS paradigm, the dividend decisions by Islamic banks managers are subject to the interactions between PSIA and dividend distributions.

In contrast, Conventional banks are known as intermediates between depositors and borrowers, and their revenue is defined as the difference in the interest gains between the two parties. Thus, their net profit is calculated by the deduction of expenses from revenues (Saeed and Izzeldin 2016). Pay-out decisions in Conventional banks, nevertheless, are related to current bank profitability, future growth opportunities and optimal capital budget as well as the equity amount needed to finance the optimal budget via retained earnings (see Partington 1989; Deshmukh et al. 2013; Onali et al. 2016).

Such detailed process between two bank types implies a more complicated dividend pay-out model in Islamic banks, as compared to Conventional banks. This is empirically supported by Athari et al. (2016) and Trinh et al. (2021).

References

Abdelsalam, O., P. Dimitropoulos, M. Elnahass, and S. Leventis. 2016. Earnings management behaviors under different monitoring mechanisms: The case of Islamic and conventional banks. *Journal of Economic Behavior & Organization* 132: 155–173.

Abedifar, P., P. Molyneux, and A. Tarazi. 2013. Risk in Islamic banking. *Review of Finance* 17 (6): 2035–2096.
Aggarwal, R.K., and T. Yousef. 2000. Islamic banks and investment financing. *Journal of Money, Credit and Banking*: 93–120.
Ahmed, E.T.A. 1996. Distribution of profits in Islamic banking: a case study of Faysal Islamic Bank of Sudan (FIBS). *Journal of King Abdulaziz University: Islamic Economics* 8: 15–32.
Akhtar, S. 2007. Building an effective Islamic financial system. *BIS Review* 38: 1–7.
Alhabshi, S.M. 2002. Financial Performance Measurement and Distribution Policy of Islamic Financial Institutions. *IIUM Journal of Economics and Management* 10 (1): 2.
Al-Hunnayan, S.A.Y.E.D, and Hashem, A.. 2011. *The payout policy in the GCC: The case of Islamic banks* (Doctoral dissertation, Durham University).
Alnasser, A.S., and J. Muhammed. 2012. Introduction to corporate governance from Islamic perspective. *Humanomics* 28 (3): 220–231.
Al-Rai, 2010. Electronic banking and safety precaution. *Newspaper.*
Archer, S., and R.A.A. Karim eds., 2002. *Islamic Finance: Innovation and Growth.* Euromoney books.
———. 2006. On capital structure, risk sharing and capital adequacy in Islamic banks. *International Journal of Theoretical and Applied Finance* 9 (03): 269–280.
———. 2009. Profit-sharing investment accounts in Islamic banks: Regulatory problems and possible solutions. *Journal of Banking Regulation* 10 (4): 300–306.
Archer, S., R.A.A. Karim, and T. Al-Deehani. 1998. Financial contracting, governance structures and the accounting regulation of Islamic banks: an analysis in terms of agency theory and transaction cost economics. *Journal of Management and Governance* 2 (2): 149–170.
Askari, H., Z. Iqbal, and A. Mirakhor. 2010. *Globalization and Islamic finance: Convergence, prospects and challenges* (Vol. 778). Wiley.
Athari, S.A., C. Adaoglu, and E. Bektas. 2016. Investor protection and dividend policy: The case of Islamic and conventional banks. *Emerging Markets Review* 27: 100–117.
Aysan, A.F., M. Disli, A. Ng, and H. Ozturk. 2016. Is small the new big? Islamic banking for SMEs in Turkey. *Economic Modelling* 54: 187–194.
Ayub, M. 2007. *Understanding Islamic Finance.* Singapore: Wiley.
Bacha, O.I. 1996. Conventional versus mudarabah financing: An agency cost perspective. *International Journal of Economics, Management and Accounting*, *4*(1&2).
Bashir, B.A. 1983. Portfolio management of Islamic banks:'Certainty model'. *Journal of Banking & Finance* 7 (3): 339–354.
Beck, T., A. Demirguc-Kunt, and O. Merrouche. 2013. Islamic vs. conventional banking: Business model, efficiency, and stability. *Journal of Banking & Finance* 37: 433–447.
Beekun, R.I., and J.A. Badawi. 2005. Balancing ethical responsibility among multiple organizational stakeholders: The Islamic perspective. *Journal of Business Ethics* 60 (2): 131–145.
Belal, A.R., O. Abdelsalam, and S.S. Nizamee. 2015. Ethical Reporting in Islami Bank Bangladesh Limited (1983–2010). *Journal of Business Ethics* 129 (4): 769–784.
Bitar, M., P. Madiès, and O. Taramasco. 2017. What makes Islamic banks different? A multivariate approach. *Economic Systems* 41 (2): 215–235.
Bowie, N.E., and R.E. Freeman. 1992. *Ethics and agency theory: An introduction.* Oxford University Press.
Chapra, M.U., and H. Ahmed. 2002. *Corporate governance in Islamic financial institutions.* Jeddah: Islamic Development Bank.
Choudhury, M.A., and M.N. Alam. 2013. Corporate governance in Islamic perspective. *International Journal of Islamic and Middle Eastern Finance and Management* 6 (3): 180–199.
Claessens, S. 2006, April. Corporate Governance of Islamic Banks: Why is Important, How is it Special and What does this Imply?. In *Conference on Islamic Finance: Challenges and Opportunities', World Bank Financial Sector Network and Islamic Financial Services Board, World Bank, Washington, DC* (Vol. 24).

Dar, H.A., and J.R. Presley. 2000. Lack of profit loss sharing in Islamic banking: management and control imbalances. *International journal of Islamic financial services* 2 (2): 3–18.
Deng, S., E. Elyasiani, and C.X. Mao. 2017. Derivatives-hedging, risk allocation and the cost of debt: Evidence from bank holding companies. *The Quarterly Review of Economics and Finance* 65: 114–127.
Deshmukh, S., A.M. Goel, and K.M. Howe. 2013. CEO overconfidence and dividend policy. *Journal of Financial Intermediation* 22 (3): 440–463.
Diamond, D.W., and P.H. Dybvig. 1983. Bank runs, deposit insurance, and liquidity. *Journal of Political Economy* 91 (3): 401–419.
Diamond, D.W., and R.G. Rajan. 2001. Liquidity risk, liquidity creation, and financial fragility: A theory of banking. *Journal of Political Economy* 109 (2): 287–327.
Diamond, D.W. 1984. Financial intermediation and delegated monitoring. *The Review of Economic Studies* 51 (3): 393–414.
El-Hawary, D., W. Grais, and Z. Iqbal. 2007. Diversity in the regulation of Islamic financial institutions. *The Quarterly Review of Economics and Finance* 46 (5): 778–800.
Elnahass, M., M. Izzeldin, and O. Abdelsalam. 2014. Loan loss provisions, bank valuations and discretion: A comparative study between conventional and Islamic banks. *Journal of Economic Behavior & Organization* 103: S160–S173.
Elnahass, M., M. Izzeldin, and G. Steele. 2018. Capital and Earnings Management: Evidence from Alternative Banking Business Models. *The International Journal of Accounting* 53 (1): 20–32.
Emirates Islamic Bank. 2009. Annual report 2009.
Fama, E.F., and M.C. Jensen. 1983. Agency problems and residual claims. *The Journal of Law and Economics* 26 (2): 327–349.
Fama, E.F. 1980. Agency problems and the theory of the firm. *Journal of Political Economy* 88 (2): 288–307.
Farag, H., C. Mallin, and K. Ow-Yong. 2018. Corporate governance in Islamic banks: New insights for dual board structure and agency relationships. *Journal of International Financial Markets, Institutions and Money* 54: 59–77.
Farook, S., M.K. Hassan, and G. Clinch. 2012. Profit distribution management by Islamic banks: An empirical investigation. *The Quarterly Review of Economics and Finance* 52 (3): 333–347.
Gambling, T.E., and R.A.A. Karim. 1986. Islam and 'social accounting'. *Journal of Business Finance & Accounting* 13 (1): 39–50.
Gooden, S. 2001. Participation of stakeholders in the corporate governance of Islamic financial institutions. *New Horizon* 114: 12–15.
Grais, W., and M. Pellegrini. 2006. *Corporate governance in institutions offering Islamic financial services: Issues and options*. The World Bank.
Haniffa, R., and M. Hudaib. 2007. Exploring the ethical identity of Islamic banks via communication in annual reports. *Journal of Business Ethics* 76 (1): 97–116.
Hart, S.L. 1995. A natural-resource-based view of the firm. *Academy of Management Review* 20 (4): 986–1014.
Hasan, M., and J. Dridi. 2011. The effects of the global crisis on Islamic and conventional banks: A comparative study. *Journal of International Commerce, Economics and Policy* 2 (02): 163–200.
Hasan, Z. 2009. Corporate governance: Western and Islamic perspectives. *International Review of Business Research Papers* 5 (1): 277–293.
Hassan, K.M., J.B. Farhat, and B. Al-Zu'bi. 2003. Dividend signaling hypothesis and short-term asset concentration of Islamic interest-free banking. *Islamic Economic Studies* 11 (1).
Iqbal, M., and D.T. Llewellyn, eds. 2002. *Islamic banking and finance: new perspectives on profit sharing and risk*. Edward Elgar Publishing.
Jensen, M.C., and C.L. Smith. 1985. Stockholder, manager and creditor interests: applications of agency theory. In *Recent Advances in Corporate Finance*, ed. E.I. Altman and M.G. Subrahmanyam. Homewoord, IL: Irwin.
Jensen, M.C., and W.H. Meckling. 1976. Theory of the firm: Managerial behavior, agency costs and ownership structure. *Journal of Financial Economics* 3 (4): 305–360.

Kettell, B. 2011. *Introduction to Islamic banking and finance* (Vol. 1). Wiley.
Khalaf, R. 2007. *Islamic Banking Seeks Global Standards*, Ft.com. [online] Available at: https://www.ft.com/content/75249f32-95df-11dc-b7ec-0000779fd2ac. [Accessed 28 Dec. 2016].
Khan, M., and A. Mirakhor. 1989. The financial system and monetary policy in an Islamic economy. *Journal of King Abdulaziz University: Islamic Economics* 1 (1).
Khediri, K.B., L. Charfeddine, and S.B. Youssef. 2015. Islamic versus conventional banks in the GCC countries: A comparative study using classification techniques. *Research in International Business and Finance* 33: 75–98.
La Porta, R., F. Lopez-de-Silanes, and A. Shleifer. 1999. Corporate ownership around the world. *The Journal of Finance* 54 (2): 471–517.
Lewis, M.K. 2008. In what ways does Islamic banking differ from conventional finance? *Journal of Islamic Economics, Banking and Finance* 4 (3): 9–24.
Malkawi, B.H. 2013. Shari'ah Board in the Governance Structure of Islamic Financial Institutions. *The American Journal of Comparative Law* 61 (3): 539–578.
Mallin, C., H. Farag, and K. Ow-Yong. 2014. Corporate social responsibility and financial performance in Islamic banks. *Journal of Economic Behavior & Organization* 103: S21–S38.
McMillen, M.J. 2006. Islamic capital markets: developments and issues. *Capital Markets Law Journal* 1 (2): 136–172.
Mills, P., and J. Presley. 1999. *Islamic finance: Theory and practice*. Springer.
Mollah, S., and M. Zaman. 2015. Shari'ah supervision, corporate governance and performance: Conventional vs. Islamic banks. *Journal of Banking & Finance* 58: 418–435.
Mollah, S., M.K. Hassan, O. Al Farooque, and A. Mobarek. 2017. The governance, risk-taking, and performance of Islamic banks. *Journal of Financial Services Research* 51 (2): 195–219.
Nienhaus, V. 2007. Governance of Islamic banks. *Handbook of Islamic banking* 1: 129.
Obaidullah, M. 2005. Islamic financial services.
Olson, D., and T.A. Zoubi. 2008. Using accounting ratios to distinguish between Islamic and conventional banks in the GCC region. *The International Journal of Accounting* 43 (1): 45–65.
Onali, E., R. Galiakhmetova, P. Molyneux, and G. Torluccio. 2016. CEO power, government monitoring, and bank dividends. *Journal of Financial Intermediation* 27: 89–117.
Partington, G.H. 1989. Variables influencing dividend policy in Australia: Survey results. *Journal of Business Finance & Accounting* 16 (2): 165–182.
Quttainah, M.A., L. Song, and Q. Wu. 2013. Do Islamic banks employ less earnings management? *Journal of International Financial Management & Accounting* 24 (3): 203–233.
Rammal, H.G. 2006. The importance of Shari'ah supervision in Islamic financial institutions. *Corporate Ownership and Control* 3 (3): 204–208.
Saeed, M., and M. Izzeldin. 2016. Examining the relationship between default risk and efficiency in Islamic and conventional banks. *Journal of Economic Behavior & Organization* 132: 127–154.
Safieddine, A. 2009. Islamic financial institutions and corporate governance: New insights for agency theory. *Corporate Governance: An International Review* 17 (2): 142–158.
Safiullah, M., and A. Shamsuddin. 2019. Risk-adjusted efficiency and corporate governance: Evidence from Islamic and conventional banks. *Journal of Corporate Finance* 55: 105–140.
Schaik, V.D. 2001. Islamic banking. *The Arab Bank Review* 3 (1): 45–52.
Shibani, O., and C. De Fuentes. 2017. Differences and similaritites between corporate governance principles in Islamic banks and Conventional banks. *Research in International Business and Finance* 42: 1005–1010.
Townsend, R.M. 1979. Optimal contracts and competitive markets with costly state verification. *Journal of Economic Theory* 21 (2): 265–293.
Trinh, V.Q., M. Elnahass, and A. Salama. 2021. Board busyness and new insights into alternative bank dividends models. *Review of Quantitative Finance and Accounting* 56 (4): 1289–1328.
Van Greuning, H., and Z. Iqbal. 2008. *Risk analysis for Islamic banks*. World Bank Publications.
Zaher, T.S., and K.M. Hassan. 2001. A comparative literature survey of Islamic finance and banking. *Financial Markets, Institutions & Instruments* 10 (4): 155–199.

Chapter 5
Board Busyness Hypotheses for Banks

5.1 Board of Directors' Busyness in Dual Banking System

Governance of Banking institutions is unique due to the high complexity of this industry and the different structure of bank balance sheet (Macey and O'hara 2003; Adams and Mehran 2003). Such uniqueness of governance implies a dominant influence of the boards of directors on a bank's stability such as accounting-based and market-based performance, risk indicators, as well as corporate policies (Adams and Mehran 2003; Elyasiani and Zhang 2015; Trinh et al. 2020b, 2021b; Elnahass et al. 2020). It is therefore imperative to explore such relationships in the banking sector in that the boards are particularly essential for banks due to their complexities, intense information asymmetries, opaqueness and contracting peculiarities (Leventis et al. 2013). Effective scrutiny and advisory services from boards are indispensable to achieving and enhancing the public trust and confidence in the whole banking system, which is crucial to the proper functioning of the banking industry and the global economy. In contrast, ineffective boards may lead to the failure of banks, which can generate significant public costs[1] and consequences because of their potential effect on any deposit insurance scheme, contagion risk and payment systems. Ineffective boards may also lead investors to lose their confidence in the ability of banks to properly manage their assets and liabilities; and hence could cause liquidity crisis.

As mentioned previously and in line with agency perspective, a board of directors is viewed as a professional referee (Fama 1980) which serves as one of the monitoring agents that has a legal and moral obligation in aligning manager and shareholder interests to ensure that businesses are run in the best interests of shareholders

[1] Significant costs occur due to the special nature of banks involving in their distinctive roles in financial intermediation, the payments system, liquidity, information, and maturity and denomination transformation (Fama 1985).

V. Quang Trinh, *Fundamentals of Board Busyness and Corporate Governance*, Contributions to Management Science,
https://doi.org/10.1007/978-3-030-89228-9_5

(Fama and Jensen 1983; Harris and Shimizu 2004; Monks and Minow 2011). The function of this board can be expressed, in a complementary fashion, through: (i) the control role, informed by agency theory; and (ii) the strategy and service roles, as informed by resource dependence theory (Pfeffer and Salancik 1978; Hillman and Dalziel 2003; Brennan et al. 2016).

Furthermore, boards accommodate inside and affiliated members, including senior managers, as well as outside directors.

On the one hand, insiders have unique business knowledge which outsiders do not have (i.e., information asymmetry—Brennan et al. 2016), provide valuable information about the institution's activities (Byrd and Hickman 1992; Chapra and Ahmed 2002), but are influenced by CEO power (Mollah and Zaman 2015). From an agency perspective, information is regarded as a commodity and the board of directors, therefore, gets its authority to control and monitor managerial opportunism (Eisenhardt 1989).

On the other hand, outsiders are expected to provide vigilant oversight over executives and perform their duties independently from them (Chapra and Ahmed 2002). They should serve as the real monitors on the board on behalf of capital providers (Fama and Jensen 1983; Byrd and Hickman 1992) and, therefore, are expected to mitigate agency conflicts (Jensen and Meckling 1976; Fama and Jensen 1983).

Firms interested in improving growth and return to shareholders should avoid boards dominated by insiders and should pay careful attention to the selection of 'resource-rich' outsiders who can provide invaluable environmental linkages (Boyd 1990). Pathan (2009) also report that independent directors in bank holding companies are associated with less risk-taking, suggesting that they may view their responsibilities, roles and functions as balancing the interests of owners and other external stakeholders such as bank depositors and regulators.

As discussed previously, multiple directorships of outside directors in companies have recently become a subject of academic debate. They are not only observed as a positive indicator for benefits of directors, but also as a negative sign for the risks of directors being stretched thin. This appears two competing hypotheses on the outcomes of companies with "busy" boards—Reputation and Busyness Hypothesis.

The former postulates that the number of outside board seats held by directors, as a proxy for their reputation capital in the external labour market (Vafeas 1999), is related to their managerial performance as monitoring specialists (Fich and Shivdasani 2006). As such, multiple board appointments can signal director quality (Fama and Jensen 1983) and may improve board decision making ability and lead to a positive performance by firms for which directors hold more outside board seats (Ahn et al. 2010). These directors can be a source of valuable knowledge, experience, and business connections, and hence they can provide better advice (Haunschild 1993; Zajac and Westphal 1996; Haunschild and Beckman 1998; Harris and Shimizu 2004). If this is the case, we expect that these directors can help in increasing the level of board monitoring, lessening agency costs, and protecting shareholder interests.

Conversely, there is an overwhelmingly strong opposite view, the Busyness Hypothesis. This hypothesis predicts an inverse relation between the board's busyness and the firm's performance (and a positive association with firm risk) (Ahn et al. 2010; Cooper and Uzun 2012). It claims that accumulation of board seats over-commits a director (Fich and Shivdasani 2006; Jiraporn et al. 2008; Jackling and Johl 2009; Cashman et al. 2012; Falato et al. 2014; Zhang 2016). Directors who serve on multiple boards become so busy that they are unable to monitor management effectively.

Financial institutions, in particular banks, are different from non-financial firms as they have unique governance structures (Adams and Mehran 2003).

- First, they are perceived to be opaque and more complex than industrial firms (Levine 2004). Although information asymmetry challenges all sectors, the problems arising for banking firms may be aggravated due to their complex businesses (Furfine 2001; Levine 2004; Morgan 2002). Complexity or opacity makes difficulties for outside stakeholders to scrutinise bank activities because of its reflection to the bank's idiosyncratic nature (Andres and Vallelado 2008). It may take the forms of loan quality (not readily observable), financial engineering (not being transparent), financial statements (complicated), investment risk (being easily modified), or perquisites that managers/insiders are easier to achieve (Levine 2004). Therefore, it greatly aggravates issues involved in bank governance. Management of complexity would require more effective scrutiny of boards towards managers and more valuable advice to run the bank operations.
- Second, the banking sector is characterised by an industry which has stricter regulatory structure and more debt using level. It is very potential for the contagion within banking institutions as well as from those banks to the whole financial system and real economy (Elyasiani and Zhang 2015). For example, they are heavily regulated and are subject to supervisory actions; and they are highly leveraged due to customers' deposits (normally are financed by 90 percent or more debt) (Macey and O'hara 2003). Last but not least, bank board of directors often have larger size with more outside directors, suggesting that banks perceive a high need for advising relatively compared to non-financial firms (Pathan and Skully 2010; Adams and Mehran 2003). Recruiting "busy" outside directors in banks' board of directors are expected to not only bring in more valuable skills, knowledge and experience to provide better advising services but also mitigate the free-rider and coordination costs of large boards. "Busy" directors may also help the banking firms to widen their community relationships and thus, can obtain more business through broader networking

In line with prior studies (e.g., Elyasiani and Zhang 2015; Trinh et al. 2020b, 2021a, b; Elnahass et al. 2020), it could be expected that banks globally have become increasingly complex and opaque due to the advancement of technology, their involvement in securities trading and an increasing trend of off-balance sheet activities, and hence, requiring more advising from their board of directors. The board must be responsible for approving the banks' major policies, procedures, and business strategies and the ultimate oversight responsibility for its risk-taking decisions (e.g., default risk and credit risk). Therefore, the existence of "busy" outside directors tends to improve the operating performance and control the risk of the banks.

Moreover, firms with relatively lower agency problems are likely to benefit more from the valuable resource provided by "busy" outsiders, who can bring their considerable knowledge, experience, talent, and business connections as evidenced by their reputation in the labour market (Chen 2008). If this is the case, then apparently the cost of ineffective monitoring could be offset, and a positive relationship may exist between multi-directorships and firm performance.

However, "busy" independent directors may not have the reputation and networking contacts that are necessary to generate benefits to the institution (Jackling and Johl 2009). It is commonly agreed that "busy" directors have been criticised for being ineffective and that a reduction in their workload is associated with improved operating profits and higher market-to-book ratios (Hauser 2018). To competently contribute and effectively discharge monitoring responsibilities, they are required to spend a lot more time in board meetings (Trinh et al. 2021b).

According to Chen (2008), "busy" directors have differing impacts on the performance of firms depending on the level of agency conflicts associated with the firm's operations. Considering the dual oversight and resource roles of directors, the value of multiple directorships depends on the relative importance of monitoring as well as the resources expected from outsiders. Therefore, if the need for monitoring is crucial for certain types of organisations, due to the higher complexities and uniqueness of agency problems, the oversight role of outsiders is relatively more important than their resource function.

Within the context of Islamic banking, agency-principle relationships are more complex when compared to conventional counterparts (Safieddine 2009). Religious, social norms (i.e., values extracted from religious texts), that extend the moral accountability constraints of banks' actors (managers, SSB members, and board of directors) beyond their legal liability are likely to reduce agency costs in religiously oriented banks (Abdelsalam et al. 2016). Social norms refer to the external rules and values shared by a group of individuals. Individuals are expected to comply with the understandings and reactions of their peer groups to avoid sanctions associated with non-adherence to the common values and beliefs. Accepted attitudes are likely to be widely supported and socially approved by the community (Leventis et al. 2013).

However, the distinct nature of the bank-depositor relationship in Islamic banks is likely to promote additional complexities to the agency costs associated with this banking sector. While depositors receive fixed rate of return (interest) on investments in the conventional banking system, Islamic banks use the profit-sharing contract to invest funds on behalf of investment account holders (IAHs) who earn their returns by sharing in the profits generated from their funds, and bear their share in any investment losses incurred. In practice, IAHs have no right to intervene in the financial and operating management of their funds and do not have the benefit of a board of directors to monitor management on their behalf (Abdel Karim 2001). Therefore, Islamic banks' managers have opportunities to pursue their personal benefits at the expense of IAHs (Safieddine 2009) resulting in additional agency costs to be carried by the depositors (Abdelsalam et al. 2016).

In such context of high-level of agency costs in Islamic banks and the importance of high monitoring and oversight, a study in board busyness in Islamic banking sector could conjecture that "busy" board of directors would be less able to provide the necessary level of oversight. Thus, the pitfall associated with less effective monitoring can lead to poor performance, and high risk in Islamic banks as managers can pursue their self-interest at the expense of IAHs. With the higher complexities and uniqueness of the institutional characteristics in the special context of Islamic banks (Safieddine 2009), together with the momentousness of opting for qualified directors to oversee executives (which can result in a possible shortage of outsiders with much needed unique expertise), studies could expect that time constraint imposed by their "busy" board of directors would produce greater agency costs, worsen board monitoring quality, and will adversely affect the bank operating performance and induce additional risk-taking behaviour in comparison to their conventional counterparts.

5.2 Shari'ah Governance Busyness in Islamic Banks

While the "*single-layer*" governance mechanism in conventional banks suggests that they are not dominated by religious preoccupations and, therefore, board of directors in conventional banks is more independent on its decision-making process than in Islamic counterparts, the presence of an "*extra layer*" of governance—board of directors in Islamic banks could serve as an effective mechanism to monitor Islamic banks' prioritisation of religious, social norms.[2] The presence of SSB, therefore, tends to play a catalytic role in promoting public acceptance for this banking industry.

In line with the *Reputation Hypothesis*, we can predict that popular Shari'ah scholars own valuable skills, business connections, and built-up knowledge gained from different management strategies they have learned and practised in other contexts (Carpenter and Westphal 2001; Perry and Peyer 2005; Elyasiani and Zhang 2015). As such, SSB capital properties—human (experience, expertise, reputation) and social (networking with other banks and external organisations)—can support the overall performance of their Islamic banks. Moreover, employing popular Shari'ah scholars is expected to add credibility for the Shari'ah-compliant practices of their Islamic banks. This is likely to have implications for investors and IAHs who might be attracted to invest in these Islamic banks on the ground of high trust in their business practices. Therefore, the expertise and reputation of Shari'ah

[2] Such social norms in Islamic banks fulfil the religious obligation of trust (*Amana*), which requires the banks' actors to behave per the principles of justice (*Adl*), balance (*Qist*), and perfection (*Ihsaan*) (Beekun and Badawi 2005).

supervisors with multiple directorships might offer some positive contributions to the business success of Islamic banks while attenuating complex agency costs. This stimulates better financial positions by scrutinising risk-taking activities for Islamic banks.

Apparently, the scarcity of experts in Shari'ah law on a global basis, together with the absence of specific regulatory guidelines and the lack of clarity in assessing the performance of the SSB, might constitute major obstacles against ensuring good Shari'ah governance. In practice, Shari'ah advisors and outside directors in Islamic banks tend to be overcommitted across several banks, countries or even continents. Therefore, their limited efforts and attention can have an adverse impact on their monitoring function and, hence, inducing additional agency costs to an Islamic bank. Moreover, large salaries and commissions paid to SSB members, due to operational and contractual complexities, would contribute to increasing operating expenses leading to possible lower cost efficiency (Brick et al. 2006). Such barriers are substantially consistent with the busyness hypothesis and, hence, can cause bank performance and values to decline (Shivdasani and Yermack 1999; Jiraporn et al. 2009). Therefore, it can be theoretically predicted that "busy" Shari'ah supervisors are likely to encounter serious governance problems, caused by distorted monitoring functions and limited attention. According to Fich and Shivdasani (2006), companies with "busy" boards tend to experience a decline in their quality of corporate governance and display weak operating profitability. Such complications should adversely affect the bank performance and induce a high-risk profile.

5.3 Empirical Evidence

A research series of board busyness in relation to stability, policies and financial outcomes of dual banking system has been published in recent years. The following shows the summary of these studies.

5.3.1 Study 1: "Board Busyness, Performance and Financial Stability: Does Bank Type Matter?" (2020)

The first is of Trinh et al. (2020b) who investigate the effect of a "busy" board of directors on the firm performance and risks in a dual banking system (i.e., Islamic versus conventional banks). Their sample includes banks listed in fourteen countries over six years from 2010. They find that for the full sample including two types of banks, banks with the presence of "busy" board directors tend to exhibit high financial performance and low risk-taking behaviour (that is, high profitability, low cost to income and low insolvency and credit risk). As mentioned previously, they claim that the recruitment of "busy" directors could bring the banks several benefits such as rich experience, expertise, networking and other resources. This could in turn increase the quality of board-level decision-making and enhance the efficiency of resources utilisation as well as a monitoring function. Their evidence for the whole sample supports the resource dependence theory and hence, the reputation hypothesis.

Nevertheless, their additional analyses on different banking types (Islamic vs conventional) reveal interesting results which are consistent with the expectations presented in Sects. 5.1 and 5.2 above. Specifically, they find that reputational benefits obtained from "busy" directors are more intensified for conventional banks than for their Islamic peers. Performance and risk indicators in Islamic banks are adversely influenced by board (both the regular board of directors and SSB) busyness (lower performance and higher risk). The main argument that they reported is the complication of Islamic banks in terms of business models, corporate governance and agency problems, which leads to a higher demand for additional monitoring effectiveness from boards. The uniqueness of their financial products within the Islamic banking sector could be also the reason. It is noted that "busy" boards are more likely to relate to less time and attention leading to lower monitoring effectiveness.

Reference Trinh V.Q., Elnahass M., Salama A., Izzeldin M., 2020. Board Busyness, Performance and Financial Stability: Does Bank Type Matter? In: *European Journal of Finance*, 26 (7–8), 774–801.

5.3.2 Study 2: "Differential Market Valuations of Board Busyness Across Alternative Banking Models" (2020)

The second is of Elnahass et al. (2020) who examine whether and how market participants value the stocks of banks with "busy" boards of directors. Using the sample which includes equities of both Conventional and Islamic banking institutions listed on stock markets across eleven countries for six years from 2010, they find that board busyness is differently valued by investors engaging in Conventional and Islamic banks. For the former, they find that investors seem to highly price stocks with the presence of "busy" boards of directors probably because they perceive that these boards could possess superior knowledge of industry, establish external networks as well as facilitation of external market sources.

However, an opposing finding is found for the latter (Islamic banks). That is, they find no supporting evidence for the effects of "busy" boards on bank market valuation. This is due to the theories that Islamic banks are more complex than their Conventional peers in terms of governance structure and the uniqueness of their business model and as such, additional and effective monitoring is required. In addition, the authors also find a significant and negative association between market value and SSB busyness, implying that investors do not prefer banks with "busy" SSB. In other words, the stock market is sensitive to the busyness functions of boards: board of directors in Conventional banks and religious SSB board in Islamic banks.

Reference Elnahass M., Omoteso, K., Salama A., Trinh V.Q., 2020. Differential Market Valuations of Board Busyness across Alternative Banking Models. In: Review of Quantitative Finance and Accounting, 55, 201–238.

5.3.3 Study 3: "Fetching Better Deals from Creditors: Board Busyness, Agency Relationships and the Bank Cost of Debt" (2020)

The third is of Trinh et al. (2020a) who examine the effect of a "busy" board of directors on banks' cost of debt. They interestingly find that for the full sample, such busyness could help to enhance the financing capacity of banks through a lower cost of debt financing. This can be explained by signalling the quality hypothesis discussed earlier in Chap. 1. Their extended analysis further shows different results for different bank types. Conventional banks still obtain a consistent result which supports the beneficial effects of board busyness on the valuation of debtholders and hence, improves the rate of borrowing.

In contrast, for their Islamic counterparts, such "busy" boards reveal a negative impact which implies that the negative relationship between busyness and cost of debt is more intensified in Conventional banks than Islamic banks. Similar reasons have been given to explain the different results between two types of banks: the distinctive governance structure, agency conflicts, and the complexity of the Islamic business model have increased the monitoring effectiveness requirements from the boards. Muslim debtholders are argued to depreciate board busyness because they may believe that such attribute will not bring benefits to the board monitoring, or even lower its effectiveness in supervising. The findings in this study seem to provide a positive counterpoint to the negative association that exists between the board of directors' busyness and corporate performance. Thereby, they could subsequently contribute to the existing knowledge regarding the important role of "busy" boards of directors play in debt financing.

Reference Trinh V.Q., Al Jughaiman, A., Cao, D.N., 2020. Fetching better deals from creditors: Board busyness, agency relationships and the bank cost of debt. In: International Review of Financial Analysis, 69.

5.3.4 Study 4: "Board Busyness and New Insights into Alternative Bank Dividends Models" (2021)

The fourth is of Trinh et al. (2021b) who investigate the impacts of a "busy" board of directors on the dividend pay-out patterns between two alternative dividend models of Conventional and Islamic banks. They employ a sample of listed banks in eleven countries over the thirteen years from 2006. They find that board busyness is one of the important factors that help to explain the differential dividend pay-outs behaviour between two banking systems. That is, for the Conventional banking dividend model, banks with a "busy" board of directors tend to exhibit a higher propensity to pay cash dividends as well as a higher cash dividend pay-out level. Nevertheless, such a positive effect was tempered during the global financial crisis 2007–2009. On the contrary, Islamic banks, which are operating under a more constrained dividend model (see theories presented previously), with "busy" boards of directors would be likely to exhibit lower propensity to pay and lower levels of dividend pay-outs. The financial crisis seems not to have any significant influences on such results. They explain their findings by discussing the potential challenges for the unique agency conflicts arising from the complex pay-out model of Islamic banks (in terms of profit distribution principles, motives, mechanics and techniques, and flexibility of pay-outs). Such challenges lead to higher demand for monitoring effectiveness from the boards.

Reference Trinh V.Q., Elnahass, M., Salama, A., 2021. Board busyness and new insights into alternative bank dividends models. Review of Quantitative Finance and Accounting, 56 (4), 1289–1328.

5.3.5 Study 5: "The Value Relevance of Bank Cash Holdings: The Moderating Effect of Board Busyness" (2021)

The fifth is of Trinh et al. (2021a) who explore the value relevance of a banks' cash holding information disclosure, and more importantly, examines how board busyness could moderate such value relevance of cash levels. To address these objectives, the authors have employed a sample of 70 listed (Conventional and Islamic) banks across eleven countries for nine years from 2010. They find that for the whole sample, investors tend to negatively price the large cash flow holdings of banks average. Nonetheless, if the banks recruit "busy" board members possessing richer experience in effectively monitoring free cash flow reserves, the public confidence tends to be increased by lowering or even cancelling out the negative value relevance of cash holding information. The results found in the Islamic banking sector are different. They do not find the reputational benefits of appointing "busy" directors on the value relevance in such bank types. The reasons provided are similar to the Studies 1 to 4 above in which compared to Conventional banks, their Islamic peers have stricter monitoring by boards. This is simply because the latter has a too complicated business model, distinctive systems of governance, and more severe agency conflicts.

Reference Trinh V.Q., Elnahass, M., Cao, D.N., 2021. The Value Relevance of Bank Cash Holdings: The Moderating Effect of Board Busyness. In: Journal of International Financial Markets, Institutions and Money.

5.4 Endogeneity: A Matter in Board Busyness Research

Banking industry has the peculiar nature. Thus, they should differ in both opportunities and challenges that they may encounter over years. This leads to an endogeneity situation that board outside directorships, other board characteristics and bank outcomes are jointly and dynamically determined by unobserved bank-specific variables such as quality and style of management, business strategy, market perception and bank complexity (Guest 2009; Henry 2008). If this case happens, traditional pooled Ordinary Least Square (OLS) regressions may not be able to detect it (Kraatz and Zajac 2001; Wooldridge 2002). The assumption of OLS is that among others, the independent variables are truly exogenous that there is only one-way causation between the regress and regressor. If this is not correct, the assumption will be violated and a single equation OLS technique might give biased and inconsistent estimates. To rectify this issue, simultaneous equation models (e.g., the robust multivariate regression procedure or stage least squares) should be alternatively employed (Alih and Ong 2014).

Prior studies in board busyness literature have employed several alternative methods to minimise the endogeneity issue (e.g., Ferris et al. 2003; Field et al. 2013; Elyasiani and Zhang 2015; Elnahass et al. 2020; Trinh et al. 2020b, 2021b). Before using these approaches, they follow the two techniques as below:

1. Testing on the panel sample and use panel data analysis. *Benefit:* reduce endogeneity problems which can be arisen from potential unobserved bank-specific heterogeneity—one of three causes of endogeneity problem. Panel data (or, longitudinal data) is the data set that combine both time series and cross sections. However, panel data set are likely to be more oriented toward cross-section analysis. Panel data can help enhance the efficiency of econometric estimates by producing more accurate inference of model parameters (Hsiao 1995); higher capacity for capturing the complexity of human behaviour than a single cross-section or time series data (e.g., controlling the influence of omitted variables); and simplifying computation and statistical inference (e.g., analysis of nonstationary time series can be simplified if panel data are available and observations among cross-sectional units are independent (see Baltagi and Kao 2001; Levin et al. 2002; Im et al. 2003). However, the main challenge of panel data analysis is to control the influence of unobserved heterogeneity to obtain valid inference on the structural parameters (Hsiao 2007).

2. Employing a comprehensive set of control factors that can potentially influence dependent variables in their empirical models. *Benefit:* reduce the probability of the presence of omitted variables—one of three causes of endogeneity problem.

However, these two ways still cannot fully address endogeneity problem that is caused by the following reason: Independent variables in the model (e.g., board busyness) are likely to be determined simultaneously with dependent variables (i.e., bank outcomes) leading to a possible simultaneity bias. Random-effect GLS technique could be also become biased and inconsistent estimation if the unobserved variables are correlated with explanatory ones in the regression. First-differences or the fixed-effects (within) are also inconsistent and have different probability limits because board structure may be endogenous (Hermalin and Weisbach 1988, 1998, 2003). Therefore, empirical research in this field will need to find an alternative method which utilises instrumental variables (IVs) to cope with endogeneity problem (Wooldridge 2002). Therefore, the following most common methods could be used:

1. The Two-step System Generalized Method of Moments (GMM) estimation
2. The Two-Stage Least-Square (2SLS) estimation
3. The Three-Stage Least-Square (3SLS) estimation (*Discussed in this book*)

5.4.1 What Is the 3SLS Compared to 2SLS?

This book focuses on the Three-Stage Least-Square (3SLS) estimations because it is the most advanced method to treat endogeneity problem, among the above three common ones. As defined by Zellner and Theil (1962):

- 3SLS is regarded as a system technique which is applied to all the equations of the empirical models at the same time and gives simultaneously estimates of all the parameters. The method 3SLS is, thus, viewed as a logical extension of two stage least square (2SLS) or specifically, the combination of 2SLS and Seemingly Unrelated Regressions (SUR). It is employed in a system of simultaneous equations which are endogenous. It involves the application of the method of least square in three successive stages (Koutsoyiannis 2001).
- The first two stages are the same as 2SLS except the reduced form of all the equations of the system and hence, they refer to the first 2SLS part. In each equation, there are endogenous variables on both the left- and right-hand sides of the equation. However, the error terms in each equation can be also correlated to each other, thus the method needs to take account of this to obtain an efficient estimation. This part is the SUR. This third stage theoretically involves the application of generalised least square (GLS) which is seen as the application of least squares to a set of transformed equation that the transformation required might be obtained from the reduced form residuals of the previous stage.

Therefore, 3SLS is a convenient technique when the analyst aims at estimating simultaneous equation models in the presence of dynamic random effects (Zellner and Theil 1962; Arellano 1990). By taking into considerations the cross-equation correlation, this method can yield more efficient estimates for simultaneous equation system than 2SLS as well as single equation OLS while accounting for the possible endogeneity issues.

In addition, 3SLS is argued to have desirable features of leaving the auto covariance matrix of errors unrestricted, thus, the approach does not require the normal distribution of errors (Zellner and Theil 1962). This technique might be robust to the residual autocorrelation of an arbitrage form, consequently, it renders unbiased coefficients (Tamirisa and Igan 2008).

In summary, 3SLS allows the researchers to address two main issues:

(i) *the regression for equations which have endogenous variables*
(ii) *the error term is correlated with each other and with the error terms in other equations.*

More specifically, the essential advantage of 3SLS estimation method is that it allows not only the simultaneity among the bank outcomes and board busyness, but also for correlations among the error components. Hence, this estimation technique is believed to be more efficient than 2SLS estimators, GMM and OLS (Mallin et al. 2014).

5.4.2 How to Make Choice of Instrumental Variables (IVs)?

The answer is simple: exploit IVs from previous literature.

In theory, the choice of IVs is critical to a consistent estimation (Mallin et al. 2014). The researchers need to seeks for suitable random IVs for their potential endogenous variable(s) that satisfies two conditions (Elyasiani and Jia 2008):

1. *(a) Correlated with the suspected endogenous variable (predicting reasonably the endogenous variable)*
2. *(b) Uncorrelated with the error terms of the dependent variable.*

It is often easy to find an IV factor that satisfies (a) OR (b). However, identifying IVs that meet BOTH criteria—(a) and (b)—for the predicted endogenous variable is very challenging. In particular:

- (b) is generally not verifiable because error term is unobserved. Thus, the researchers have to argue for the validity of (b) on the ground of economic intuition.
- To verify (a), it is simply to run a simple linear regression including endogenous variable (dependent variable) and selected IVs (independent variables).

An illustrated example:

Motivated by theoretical framework and the extant literature on the board busyness, two main IVs for "busy" boards of directors are chosen by some previous studies (Elnahass et al. 2020; Trinh et al. 2021b).

- The first IV: the number of public firms headquartered in the same country/cities of the bank. *Reason:* directors of the bank headquartered in countries/cities with more public firms tend to find more jobs in other institutions and might also work in different cities across the country. It can be thereby predicted that the number of "busy" directors is positively associated with the number of public firms headquartered in the same country/city.
- The second IV: the country-level income generating category. It is a dummy variable taking a value of one if the "home" bank is in a country classified as a middle and high-income generating nation, and zero otherwise. *Reason:* a developed economic system with high level of income is likely to have increased skilled and high-paying job opportunities for directors (World Bank 2016). Highly skilled and reputable directors with professional knowledge in those nations, therefore, can easily find job opportunities through accessing open labour markets. As a result, directors of banks headquartered in high-income countries with more skill-job opportunities are more likely to find director positions in other companies. This is anticipated to positively influence the number of the directorships they hold.
- The third IV: The year-average of board busyness variable of other banks in the same country. This is a common instrumenting technique employed by a number of prior research in the field (e.g., Anginer et al. 2014; Safiullah and Shamsuddin 2019). *Reason:* it is contended that a change in the outcome of one bank is less likely to have significant impacts on the board busyness degrees of other banks.

No IVs are perfect. However, the authors can generally argue that the above IVs are expected to be (a) correlated with the potential endogenous variable (board busyness), and at the same time (b) be less likely to correlated with unobserved factors that affect dependent variables (e.g., financial stability, market valuations and other outcomes of individual banks).

It can be supposed that there exists slight correlation between the IVs and the residual, the IV estimators might be asymptotically biased. This bias could be severe if the correlation between the IVs and the endogenous variable is low. Therefore, to avoid large asymptotic bias, empirical studies need to attempt to choose IVs that are more correlated with the endogenous variable (board busyness). The above IVs should satisfy the necessary conditions for valid instruments which assumes that the disturbance is not auto-correlated (Kennedy 2003). Such assumption is tested by using both the Breusch-Godfrey-Lagrange Multiplier and Durbin-Watson tests (Mallin et al. 2014). The results of both tests indicate that the residuals are not serially correlated.

The advantage of 3SLS depends on validity of IVs and the correct specification of the system (Beiner et al. 2006). Each study should perform two diagnostic tests to identify the validity of both the IVs and the specification of the system equations (see Mallin et al. 2014):

1. *The Breusch and Pagan Lagrange Multiplier (LM) test:* to examine whether cross-equation disturbances are truly associated and if the equations need to be tested simultaneously (Breusch and Pagan 1980). The results of the LM test should indicate that cross-equation residuals were not independent (all p-values should be lower than 0.01, 0.05 or 0.1) and if so, the test rejects the null hypothesis of independence errors which implies that the equations need to be examined simultaneously. The systems presented in all models are well-specified because the Wald Chi squared is highly significant (all Chi p-values should be less than 0.01, 0.05 or 0.1).
2. *The Sargan over-identification test:* is a misspecification test with the null hypothesis of no misspecification (Sargan 1964). The results of the Sargan misspecification test should indicate that there is no evidence to reject the null hypothesis of no misspecification, suggesting that the IVs used in the systems of the research are orthogonal to the error terms of the respective equations.

The researchers, in sum, need to ensure that their choices of IVs theoretically and statistically satisfy the necessary conditions for validity and relevance, and hence, 3SLS results tend to be consistent and more efficient than those obtained using OLS method.

5.5 Statistical Problems and Remedies

5.5.1 *Regression Diagnostic I:* Multicollinearity

Classical linear regression (CLRM), according to Gujarati and Porter (2009), assumes that there is no exact linear relationship among independent variables (or, regressors). If one or more such relationships among those variables, multicollinearity or collinearity for short will be occurred.

There are two main types of collinearity:

- *Perfect collinearity:* a perfect linear relationship between the two regressors. This leads to the omitted results.
- *Imperfect collinearity:* the regressors are highly, but not perfectly, collinear. This has several consequences, for example, one of more regression coefficients might have large standard errors relative to the values of the coefficients and hence, making the t ratios small. In addition, this high multicollinearity can make the R^2 very high although some regression coefficients are statistically insignificant. This leads to the misleading results that the true values of those coefficients are not different from zero. Also, those coefficients will be very sensitive to a small change in the data, especially in case of relatively small sample.

To detect the multicollinearity problem, the researchers could employ two different ways:

1. *Pearson correlation matrix:* result shows high pair-wise correlations among regressors
2. *Variance Inflation Factor (VIF):* is high
   OR Tolerance Factor (or the inverse of VIF): is low.

For all estimating models of any studies that are based on the panel data, the presence of multicollinearity is more likely. However, the results of the two approaches detecting multicollinearity above should indicate both, the weak (/r/ <0.3) or medium correlation (0.3</r/<0.8) among independent variables employed in all empirical models (Bernstein 1994), and low VIF values (smaller than 10) (Gujarati and Porter 2009). If these are the cases, multicollinearity might not be a concern, and hence, multicollinearity will not influence the regression results.

5.5.2 *Regression Diagnostic II:* Heteroskedasticity

Another problem, which is *heteroskedasticity,* can be often occurred during the analysis process. CLRM also assumes that the variance of the error term u_i is constant or homoscedastic. If this cannot meet, the heteroskedasticity problem will exist (Gujarati and Porter 2009). Several reasons are given:

- *The presence of outliers in the data*
- *Incorrect functional form of the regression model*
- *Incorrect transformation of data*
- *Mixing observations with different measures of scale.* This problem will make estimators less efficient and statistical inference less reliable (i.e., the estimated *t* values may not be reliable).

Hence, estimators will not be the BLUE, they are simply linear unbiased estimators (LUE) (Gujarati and Porter 2009). However, some econometrists argue that this problem is rarely occurred in panel data because the nature of panel data is to reduce heteroscedasticity. Therefore, heteroscedasticity may not be an issue for panel analysis.

However, due to the conservative purpose, future studies should also test for this problem by using both, Breusch-Pagan (BP)/Cook-Weisberg test for heteroscedasticity and White-general test (null: constant variance) (see Elnahass et al. 2018). It should find that the null hypothesis is accepted, hence, heteroscedasticity does not exist across all tested models. They should also use various methods to minimise this problem (if any) such as GMM and 2SLS with robust standard errors.

5.5.3 Regression Diagnostic III: The Simultaneity Problem and Endogeneity

In theory, exogeneity assumption of a multiple linear regression might be violated if at least one of the independent variables is correlated with the residual, hence, the regression suffers from endogeneity problem (Gujarati and Porter 2009). This problem can be occurred in three cases.

1. There is an omitted variable which is related to some independent variables.
2. There is measurement error in at least one of the independent variables.
3. The dependent variable and at least one of the independent variables are determined simultaneously in a system. Specifically, econometrists argue some situations that unidirectional relationship between dependent variable (Y) and the independent variables (Xs) cannot maintained, because some Xs affect Y but in turn Y also affects one or more Xs. In other words, a feedback relationship between Y and Xs may be exist. This is called the simultaneity problem. Simultaneous equation regression models, which are defined as models taking into considerations feedback relationships among variables, can be used to address the problem. Above Xs are called as endogenous variables which are variables whose values are determined in the model. By contrast, the remaining Xs which have no feedback relationship with Y are called as exogenous variables (or, predetermined variables) which are variables whose values are not determined in the model. Some approaches are suggested to address or minimise this problem are Method of Indirect Least Squares (ILS) or Method of Two-Stage Least Squares (2SLS), or other Instrumental Variables like 3SLS.

Endogeneity problem could be examined employing 3SLS (as the main test), 2SLS and GMM estimator for board busyness variable which is suspected to be endogenous independent variables due to simultaneity. The discussion of this potential endogeneity issue and IVs selection have been thoroughly discussed previously.

Across all models, empirical studies should perform Durbin-Wu-Hausman endogeneity test (Hausman 1978; Wooldridge 2008). The statistics of the test should indicate the presence of endogeneity bias. The null hypothesis is that the specified endogenous independent variable can actually be treated as endogenous. The test assumes selected IVs are valid instruments for board busyness. If the F-statistics report that p-values of all models are less than 1%, 5% or 10%, we could reject the null hypothesis. Therefore, "busy" board variables are endogenous and need to be solved. Therefore, it might be then concluded that 3SLS and other IV approaches are more appropriate methods than classical pooled OLS estimate. Using OLS might produce biased and inconsistent results (Mallin et al. 2014; Elyasiani and Zhang 2015; Mollah and Zaman 2015).

5.6 Measurements of Board Busyness

There are three most popular traditional proxies of "busy" boards.

1. "busy" board of directors and "busy" SSB are measured as the ratio of *outside directorships per outside director* and *outside directorships per Shari'ah advisors*, respectively. It represents the average number of other outside board seats held by each outside director/Shari'ah advisor. It is computed as the total number of additional (outside) boards occupied by outside directors/Shari'ah advisors divided by the number of outside directors/Shari'ah advisors on the board (Ferris et al. 2003). Several previous studies do not measure "busy" boards of directors as *outside directorships per director* because it can be a noisy measure of monitoring intensity as it captures busyness of both insiders and outsiders. It is believed that outside directors should be a key element of the board monitoring intensity (Fich and Shivdasani 2006). They are perceived to be better monitors of managers since they wish to maintain their reputation in the industry. They also contribute to finalise banks' strategic decisions and policies during the meetings of the boards (Pathan 2009). They are classified by bank's proxy statements relative to board size (Minton et al. 2014). Several studies, therefore, only focuses on their monitoring role in the measure of outside directorships per outside director (Jiraporn et al. 2008).
2. Based on the definition of busyness (i.e., "busy" directors are those holding at least two outside/additional directorships), many other studies also measures "busy" board of directors and "busy" SSB by the *percentage of "busy" outside directors* and the *percentage of "busy" Shari'ah advisors*. The former is the percentage of "busy" outside directors on the board, calculated as the number of outside directors serving on two or more additional (outside) firms divided by the number of outside directors on the board. The latter is the percentage of "busy" Shari'ah advisors on the board, estimated as the number of Shari'ah advisors serving on at least two additional organisations divided by the number of Shari'ah advisors on the board. The greater percentage of "busy" outside directors/Shari'ah advisors reflects higher busyness of boards which influences the monitoring quality of overall board (Ferris et al. 2003; Chakravarty and Rutherford 2017). Utilising the percentage of directors' busyness provides a plausible assessment of the board advising and monitoring intensity under the assumption of high independence, substantial contributions in the firm strategic decisions and their sound reputation maintained in the industry (Fich and Shivdasani 2006).
3. Dummy variables which take the value of 1 of at least 50% of outside directors/Shari'ah advisors are classified as "busy"directors (i.e., holds at least 2 additional board seats) (Fich and Shivdasani 2006).

The cut-off of two additional board seats (as "busy") should be revisited in future studies because: (1) the research context may be different; and (2) the number of board seats that directors hold may change over time due to the change of economic, social, technological and legal conditions.

References

Abdel Karim, R.A. 2001. International accounting harmonization, banking regulation, and Islamic banks. *The International Journal of Accounting* 36 (2): 169–193.

Abdelsalam, O., P. Dimitropoulos, M. Elnahass, and S. Leventis. 2016. Earnings management behaviors under different monitoring mechanisms: The case of Islamic and conventional banks. *Journal of Economic Behavior & Organization* 132: 155–173.

Adams, R., and H. Mehran. 2003. Is corporate governance different for bank holding companies?. *SSRN.*

Ahn, S., P. Jiraporn, and Y.S. Kim. 2010. Multiple directorships and acquirer returns. *Journal of Banking & Finance* 34 (9): 2011–2026.

Alih, E., and H.C. Ong. 2014, July. The performance of robust multivariate regression in simultaneous dependence of variables in linear models. In *AIP Conference Proceedings* (Vol. 1605, No. 1, pp. 1028–1033). AIP.

Andres, D.P., and E. Vallelado. 2008. Corporate governance in banking: The role of the board of directors. *Journal of Banking & Finance* 32 (12): 2570–2580.

Anginer, D., A. Demirgüç-Kunt, H. Huizinga, and K. Ma. 2014. Corporate governance and bank insolvency risk: International evidence.

Arellano, M. 1990. Testing for autocorrelation in dynamic random effects models. *The Review of Economic Studies* 57 (1): 127–134.

Baltagi, B.H., and C. Kao. 2001. Nonstationary panels, cointegration in panels and dynamic panels: A survey. In *Nonstationary panels, panel cointegration, and dynamic panels*. Emerald Group Publishing Limited.

Beekun, R.I., and J.A. Badawi. 2005. Balancing ethical responsibility among multiple organizational stakeholders: The Islamic perspective. *Journal of Business Ethics* 60 (2): 131–145.

Beiner, S., W. Drobetz, M.M. Schmid, and H. Zimmermann. 2006. An integrated framework of corporate governance and firm valuation. *European Financial Management* 12 (2): 249–283.

Bernstein, G.M. 1994. The variance of correlation function estimates. *The Astrophysical Journal* 424: 569–577.

Boyd, B. 1990. Corporate linkages and organizational environment: A test of the resource dependence model. *Strategic Management Journal* 11 (6): 419–430.

Brennan, N.M., C.E. Kirwan, and J. Redmond. 2016. Accountability processes in boardrooms: A conceptual model of manager-non-executive director information asymmetry. *Accounting, Auditing & Accountability Journal* 29 (1): 135–164.

Breusch, T.S., and A.R. Pagan. 1980. The Lagrange multiplier test and its applications to model specification in econometrics. *The review of economic studies* 47 (1): 239–253.

Brick, I.E., O. Palmon, and J.K. Wald. 2006. CEO compensation, director compensation, and firm performance: Evidence of cronyism? *Journal of Corporate Finance* 12 (3): 403–423.

Byrd, J.W., and K.A. Hickman. 1992. Do outside directors monitor managers?: Evidence from tender offer bids. *Journal of Financial Economics* 32 (2): 195–221.

Carpenter, M.A., and J.D. Westphal. 2001. The strategic context of external network ties: Examining the impact of director appointments on board involvement in strategic decision making. *Academy of Management Journal* 44 (4): 639–660.

Cashman, G.D., S.L. Gillan, and C. Jun. 2012. Going overboard? On busy directors and firm value. *Journal of Banking & Finance* 36 (12): 3248–3259.

Chakravarty, S., and L.G. Rutherford. 2017. Do busy directors influence the cost of debt? An examination through the lens of takeover vulnerability. *Journal of Corporate Finance* 43: 429–443.

Chapra, M.U., and H. Ahmed. 2002. *Corporate governance in Islamic financial institutions*. Jeddah: Islamic Development Bank.

Chen, C.W. 2008. *Two Essays on Multiple Directorships. University of South Florida: Graduate Theses and Dissertations*. http://scholarcommons.usf.edu/etd/171. [Accessed 15 Mar. 2017].

Cooper, E., and H. Uzun. 2012. Directors with a full plate: The impact of busy directors on bank risk. *Managerial Finance* 38 (6): 571–586.

Eisenhardt, K.M. 1989. Agency theory: An assessment and review. *Academy of Management Review* 14 (1): 57–74.

Elnahass, M., M. Izzeldin, and G. Steele. 2018. Capital and earnings management: Evidence from alternative banking business models. *The International Journal of Accounting* 53 (1): 20–32.

Elnahass, M., K. Omoteso, A. Salama, and V.Q. Trinh. 2020. Differential market valuations of board busyness across alternative banking models. *Review of Quantitative Finance and Accounting* 55 (1): 201–238.

Elyasiani, E., and J.J. Jia. 2008. Institutional ownership stability and BHC performance. *Journal of Banking & Finance* 32 (9): 1767–1781.

Elyasiani, E., and L. Zhang. 2015. Bank holding company performance, risk, and "busy" board of directors. *Journal of Banking & Finance* 60: 239–251.

Falato, A., D. Kadyrzhanova, and U. Lel. 2014. Distracted directors: Does board busyness hurt shareholder value? *Journal of Financial Economics* 113 (3): 404–426.

Fama, E.F. 1980. Agency problems and the theory of the firm. *Journal of Political Economy* 88 (2): 288–307.

———. 1985. What's different about banks? *Journal of Monetary Economics* 15 (1): 29–39.

Fama, E.F., and M.C. Jensen. 1983. Agency problems and residual claims. *The Journal of Law and Economics* 26 (2): 327–349.

Ferris, S.P., M. Jagannathan, and A.C. Pritchard. 2003. Too busy to mind the business? Monitoring by directors with multiple board appointments. *The Journal of Finance* 58 (3): 1087–1111.

Fich, E.M., and A. Shivdasani. 2006. Are busy boards effective monitors? *The Journal of Finance* 61 (2): 689–724.

Field, L., M. Lowry, and A. Mkrtchyan. 2013. Are busy boards detrimental? *Journal of Financial Economics* 109 (1): 63–82.

Furfine, C. 2001. Bank portfolio allocation: The impact of capital requirements, regulatory monitoring, and economic conditions. *Journal of Financial Services Research* 20 (1): 33–56.

Guest, P.M. 2009. The impact of board size on firm performance: Evidence from the UK. *The European Journal of Finance* 15 (4): 385–404.

Gujarati, D.N., and D.C. Porter. 2009. *Basic econometrics* (international edition). New York: McGraw-Hills.

Harris, I.C., and K. Shimizu. 2004. Too busy to serve? An examination of the influence of overboarded directors. *Journal of Management Studies* 41 (5): 775–798.

Haunschild, P.R. 1993. Interorganizational imitation: The impact of interlocks on corporate acquisition activity. *Administrative Science Quarterly* 38: 564–592.

Haunschild, P.R., and C.M. Beckman. 1998. When do interlocks matter?: Alternate sources of information and interlock influence. *Administrative Science Quarterly* 43: 815–844.

Hauser, R. 2018. Busy directors and firm performance: Evidence from mergers. *Journal of Financial Economics* 128 (1): 16–37.

Hausman, J.A. 1978. Specification tests in econometrics. *Econometrica: Journal of the Econometric Society* 46: 1251–1271.

Henry, A. 2008. *Understanding strategic management.* Oxford University Press, USA.

Hermalin, B.E., and M.S. Weisbach. 1988. The determinants of board composition. *The RAND Journal of Economics* 19: 589–606.

———. 1998. Endogenously chosen boards of directors and their monitoring of the CEO. *American Economic Review* 88: 96–118.

———. 2003. Boards of directors as an endogenously determined institution: A survey of the economic literature. *Federal Reserve Bank of New York Economic Policy Review* 9: 7–26.

Hillman, A.J., and T. Dalziel. 2003. Boards of directors and firm performance: Integrating agency and resource dependence perspectives. *Academy of Management Review* 28 (3): 383–396.

Hsiao, C. 1995. Panel analysis for metric data. In *Handbook of Statistical Modeling for the Social and Behavioral Sciences*, 361–400. Boston, MA: Springer.

———. 2007. Panel data analysis—advantages and challenges. *TEST* 16 (1): 1–22.

Im, K.S., M.H. Pesaran, and Y. Shin. 2003. Testing for unit roots in heterogeneous panels. *Journal of Econometrics* 115 (1): 53–74.

Jackling, B., and S. Johl. 2009. Board structure and firm performance: Evidence from India's top companies. *Corporate Governance: An International Review* 17 (4): 492–509.

Jensen, M.C., and W.H. Meckling. 1976. Theory of the firm: Managerial behavior, agency costs and ownership structure. *Journal of Financial Economics* 3 (4): 305–360.

Jiraporn, P., Y.S. Kim, and W.N. Davidson III. 2008. Multiple directorships and corporate diversification. *Journal of Empirical Finance* 15 (3): 418–435.

Jiraporn, P., M. Singh, and C.I. Lee. 2009. Ineffective corporate governance: Director busyness and board committee memberships. *Journal of Banking & Finance* 33 (5): 819–828.

Kennedy, P. 2003. *A Guide to Econometrics*. Cambridge, MA: MIT Press.

Koutsoyiannis, A. 2001. *Theory of Econometrics*. New York: Palgrave.

Kraatz, M.S., and E.J. Zajac. 2001. How organizational resources affect strategic change and performance in turbulent environments: Theory and evidence. *Organization Science* 12 (5): 632–657.

Leventis, S., P. Dimitropoulos, and S. Owusu-Ansah. 2013. Corporate governance and accounting conservatism: Evidence from the banking industry. *Corporate Governance: An International Review* 21 (3): 264–286.

Levin, A., C.F. Lin, and C.S.J. Chu. 2002. Unit root tests in panel data: Asymptotic and finite-sample properties. *Journal of Econometrics* 108 (1): 1–24.

Levine, R. 2004. *The Corporate Governance of Banks: A Concise Discussion of Concepts and Evidence*. The World Bank.

Macey, J., and M. O'hara 2003. The corporate governance of banks. *Economic Policy Review*, 9(1).

Mallin, C., H. Farag, and K. Ow-Yong. 2014. Corporate social responsibility and financial performance in Islamic banks. *Journal of Economic Behavior & Organization* 103: S21–S38.

Minton, B.A., J.P. Taillard, and R. Williamson. 2014. Financial expertise of the board, risk taking, and performance: Evidence from bank holding companies. *Journal of Financial and Quantitative Analysis* 49 (2): 351–380.

Mollah, S., and M. Zaman. 2015. Shari'ah supervision, corporate governance and performance: Conventional vs. Islamic banks. *Journal of Banking & Finance* 58: 418–435.

Monks, R.A.G., and N. Minow. 2011. *Corporate Governance* (5th ed.). Wiley.

Morgan, D.P. 2002. Rating banks: Risk and uncertainty in an opaque industry. *American Economic Review* 92 (4): 874–888.

Pathan, S. 2009. Strong boards, CEO power and bank risk-taking. *Journal of Banking & Finance* 33 (7): 1340–1350.

Pathan, S., and M. Skully. 2010. Endogenously structured boards of directors in banks. *Journal of Banking & Finance* 34 (7): 1590–1606.

Perry, T., and U. Peyer. 2005. Board seat accumulation by executives: A shareholder's perspective. *The Journal of Finance* 60 (4): 2083–2123.

Pfeffer, J., and G.R. Salancik. 1978. *The External Control of Organisations: A Resource Dependence Perspective*. New York: Harper & Row.

Safieddine, A. 2009. Islamic financial institutions and corporate governance: New insights for agency theory. *Corporate Governance: An International Review* 17 (2): 142–158.

Safiullah, M., and A. Shamsuddin. 2019. Risk-adjusted efficiency and corporate governance: Evidence from Islamic and conventional banks. *Journal of Corporate Finance* 55: 105–140.

Sargan, J.D. 1964. Three-stage least-squares and full maximum likelihood estimates. *Econometrica: Journal of the Econometric Society* 32: 77–81.

Shivdasani, A., and D. Yermack. 1999. CEO involvement in the selection of new board members: An empirical analysis. *The Journal of Finance* 54 (5): 1829–1853.

Tamirisa, N.T., and D.O. Igan. 2008. Are weak banks leading credit booms? Evidence from emerging Europe. *Comparative Economic Studies* 50 (4): 599–619.

Trinh, V.Q., A.A. Aljughaiman, and N.D. Cao. 2020a. Fetching better deals from creditors: Board busyness, agency relationships and the bank cost of debt. *International Review of Financial Analysis* 69: 101472.

Trinh, V.Q., M. Elnahass, A. Salama, and M. Izzeldin. 2020b. Board busyness, performance and financial stability: does bank type matter? *The European Journal of Finance* 26 (7–8): 774–801.

Trinh, V.Q., M. Elnahass, and N.D. Cao. 2021a. The value relevance of bank cash Holdings: The moderating effect of board busyness. *Journal of International Financial Markets, Institutions and Money* 73: 101359.

Trinh, V.Q., M. Elnahass, and A. Salama. 2021b. Board busyness and new insights into alternative bank dividends models. *Review of Quantitative Finance and Accounting* 56 (4): 1289–1328.

Vafeas, N. 1999. Board meeting frequency and firm performance. *Journal of Financial Economics* 53 (1): 113–142.

Wooldridge, J. 2002. *Introductory Econometrics Analysis of Cross Section and Panel Data.* London: MIT Press.

———. 2008. *Introductory Econometrics: A Modern Approach.* fourth ed. Mason, OH: South-Western College Publishing.

World Bank. 2016. *Labor market polarization in developing countries: challenges ahead.* Available at: http://blogs.worldbank.org. [Accessed 01 Aug. 2017].

Zajac, E.J., and J.D. Westphal. 1996, August. Director reputation, CEO/Board power, and the dynamics of board interlocks. In *Academy of Management Proceedings* (Vol. 1996, No. 1, pp. 254–258). Briarcliff Manor, NY 10510: Academy of Management.

Zellner, A., and H. Theil. 1962. Three-stage least squares: Simultaneous estimation of simultaneous equations. *Econometrica: Journal of the Econometric Society* 30: 54–78.

Zhang, E.J. 2016. *Preoccupied independent directors.* Working paper, UNSW Business School.

Chapter 6
Conclusions and New Direction on Board Busyness Research

This Book Covers five important areas of knowledge (Chaps. 1–5) as follows. These are presented in a summary way so that researchers and students can easily understand the theories that are relevant to corporate governance and board busyness. An unique context, i.e., the dual banking system (where both Islamic and Conventional banks are operating) is employed to better reflect the influences of such factors.

Chapter 1 presents the corporate governance theories that researchers can use to build theoretical framework when conducting their research, especially those related to corporate governance and board busyness. These theories include: agency, resource dependence, stakeholder, legitimacy, information signalling, good management, slack resource theory and behavioural theories. Only core knowledge are discussed in this chapter.

Chapter 2 presents the corporate governance in banking. In this chapter, the author discusses why governance aspects are crucial in the banking sector and what differences between their governance mechanisms and other industrial (non-financial) ones. In brief, governance in banking has been subject to an intense regulatory attention and community monitoring. Hence, there has been a growing body of empirical research focusing on various aspects of bank governance mechanisms, such as board structure/independence, CEO duality, board quality, financial expertise, busyness, compensation, and so on. All of these factors are expected to exert a significant effect on bank outcomes such as performance, risk, stability, decision-making and financial policies.

Chapter 3 presents the theories related to board busyness. They include reputation theory derived from resources dependence background and busyness theory derived from agency perspective. These theories support two opposing directions for the effect of board busyness on bank outcomes. Multiple directorships are not only observed as a positive indicator for benefits of directors, but also as a negative sign for the risks of directors being stretched thin.

Chapter 4 discusses fundamental knowledge about dual banking system, and among them, corporate governance mechanisms in two banking types (Islamic and

V. Quang Trinh, *Fundamentals of Board Busyness and Corporate Governance*, Contributions to Management Science,
https://doi.org/10.1007/978-3-030-89228-9_6

Conventional banks) are highlighted. The chapter indeed not only presents fundamentals of Islamic banking model and practice of Shari'ah governance framework, but also shows a comparison between two banking system, i.e., Islamic versus Conventional banks. Their differences could be summarised into five different areas: business model and investment modes; constraints on finance model and prohibited activities; agency conflicts; corporate governance mechanisms (single-layer governance in Conventional banks versus two-layer governance in Islamic banks); and pay-out models. In other words, Islamic banks are more complex than their Conventional peers in terms of business model, agency problem and corporate governance. Hence, the effects of governance factors on outcomes of Islamic banks should be dissimilar to those of Conventional banks.

Chapter 5 uses the fundamental knowledge in Chaps. 1, 3 and 4 to discuss board busyness hypotheses for banks. They refer to the theoretical relationship between "busy" boards (board of directors and SSB) and a bank's outcomes. Such hypotheses are built for both banking systems (Islamic and Conventional). Then, five typical and recent empirical evidence are provided to demonstrate the linkages between busyness attributes of boards and corporate outcomes in dual banking sector. An additional benefit of this chapter is to provide a guidance in conducting empirical analyses through a detailed and suggested methodology which can partly address the endogeneity problems occurred in the corporate governance and board busyness models. Future research can use this book as a guidance for their research design in this field, the topic could be either board busyness or governance in general.

Practical implications can be drawn on the effects of "busy" boards on the firm outcomes, along with remedies to handle issues imposed on the corporate governance mechanism by changes in board multiple directorships.

- An increase in the number of outside directorships hold by outside directors is expected to positively affect their ability in supervising and advising management (confirmed by empirical evidence reported in Chap. 5). Regulators and market participants in Conventional banks can benefit from these empirical evidences showing that busyness and networking of board of directors are likely to enhance bank outcomes which has implications for wealth creation.
- However, findings identifying the effect of the bank type suggest a broader and more accurate picture of board busyness' influences. The reputational benefits associated with recruiting "busy" boards might not invoke in the presence of unique institutional characteristics, as presented by the experiment of Islamic banks. Moreover, for Islamic banks, the substantial role of effective Shari'ah monitoring appears to be an essential element for promoting high stability in Islamic banks.

Furthermore, effective Shari'ah monitoring seems to be an essential determinant for enhancing outcomes of the Islamic banking sector. Therefore, the findings again raise a call to regulators and policymakers for the need to develop stricter criteria and guidelines to govern outside board directorships and SSB busyness within the Islamic banking sector. Indeed, serving in too many boards might adversely affect the responsibilities, effectiveness and risk management ability of the SSB in a complex manner. Thus, in order to improve the banking outcomes, suitable policies for Islamic banks should be established to response to an increase in overloads of SSB members and a decrease in their legal accountabilities.

Consequently, standard-setters should be cautious when deciding to adopt supposed best practices of the SSB busyness from Islamic banking environment. They should also consider the firm characteristics, institutional environment, and structural arrangement of board governance of the banks before they implement future corporate governance reforms. Previous literature suggest that all listed banks in the dual-banking countries should be required to prepare their board directorships information and disclose them to the public as such attribute might be useful to capital markets. New regulations should continue to promote board governance for the listed banks. Boards and managers should adopt high standard of future recruitment policies and of corporate governance.

Finally, I close this book by suggesting some future research and opportunities in this area. I believe that these suggestions can help researchers and students in their early research stage. They could then start thinking about their own unique ideas. Theories and hypotheses discussed in this book will be the fundamentals that they could base on to build up their own theoretical background. Interestingly, the book also discussed some basic knowledge of the methods which are common in corporate governance and board busyness research. Such techniques are useful in the context of endogeneity.

1. Future research should attempt developing empirical models including factors such as financial expertise, appropriate training and continuing education of different boards; or construct new board governance quality index.
2. Using secondary data cannot help researchers find out in-depth findings and research stories. Thus, future research can conduct survey, questionnaire or interview on outside directors and Shari'ah advisors. By doing so, they can explore new, more in-depth and interesting results; for example, the perceptions of "busy" outside directors and other stakeholders on multiple directorships, etc.
3. Future research can have opportunities to explore the effects of board busyness on other financial indicators such as managerial, financing and investing policies, risk management, accounting conservatism, innovations, corporate social responsibilities.
4. Future studies can also assess board multiple directorships under the perspectives of other stakeholders such as debtholders/creditors, suppliers and customers.

At the time this book was written, some of the suggested research topics are given in the Fig. 6.1 as below. Note that these suggestions should be conducted more innovatively to increase the contributions and implications of future research.

- The first direction is about the effect of board busyness on financing policies in a dual banking system. For this idea, authors in future studies could examine the differential effects of multiple directorships on capital structure choices of Conventional banks compared to their Islamic counterparts. To do so, they should initially explore the theoretical aspects of capital structure motives and choices of

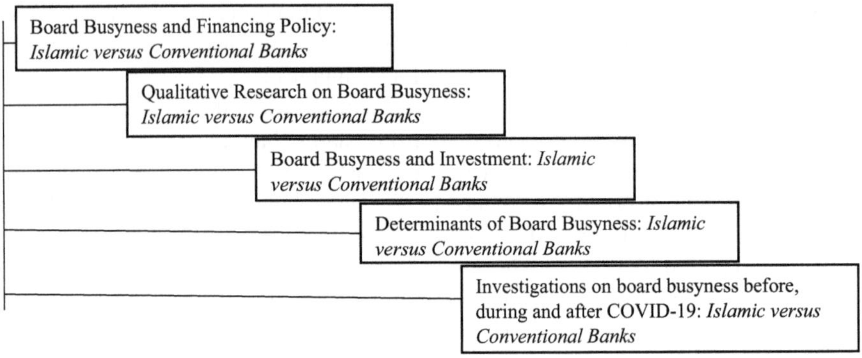

Fig. 6.1 Future research direction on board busyness (examples). *Source:* Author

two different banking models. Then they can link such differences to the context of board busyness. Several interesting findings could be found from this study.

- The second direction is a qualitative and interview study on "busy" directors including executives, non-executives, independent and non-independent directors. Existing literature only focuses on the quantitative approach and secondary data. This could not bring the readers the in-depth story about the "busy" boards and directors. Qualitative research should be conducted through a comprehensive questionnaire or survey or an interview with directors. If so, several findings from the responses of directors might be unique, novel and interesting. For example, why do directors accept multiple directorships? Are "busy" directors really "busy"? What do they think about their monitoring and advising effectiveness after taking several board seats at the same time? How could they manage their time to attend the board meetings? And so on.
- The third direction is board busyness and investment of two different banking types. The investment is reflected through innovation activities, research and development (R&D) activities, and capital expenditure. Future researchers can link the busyness function of the board of directors to the decisions of banks regarding their investment activities. For example, if the boards are busier, are their monitoring functions less effective in controlling the investment behaviour and decisions of managers?
- The fourth direction is about the determinants of "busy" directors. Current literature normally focuses on the effect of "busy" boards on corporate and bank outcomes, but we do not know much about which factors could affect the busyness attribute of directors and the boards. Therefore, a comprehensive study that exploits determinants or motives for accepting multiple directorships of directors might be very interesting.
- Last but not least, a new investigation of on board busyness before, during and after the COVID-19 pandemic crisis would be potentially an interesting research direction. In this study, future researchers could discuss how and what extent that "busy" directors can influence a bank's activities, survival likelihood, efficiency, performance, risk, etc. before and during (and perhaps after) the pandemic. Such

results can be compared with the effects of the global financial crisis 2007–2009 because these two exogenous shocks are different in nature. The reason why crises are important for examining the busyness is that the positive side of board busyness can turn to the negative side during the shock and contrast.

MIX
Papier aus verantwortungsvollen Quellen
Paper from responsible sources
FSC® C105338

If you have any concerns about our products,
you can contact us on
ProductSafety@springernature.com

In case Publisher is established outside the EU,
the EU authorized representative is:
Springer Nature Customer Service Center GmbH
Europaplatz 3, 69115 Heidelberg, Germany

Printed by Libri Plureos GmbH
in Hamburg, Germany